A Compilation of

FROM MILK TO MEAT

A Compilation Of Short Devotional Bible Studies To Guide Your Daily Walk With God

Rita Ann Bakr

My All For Jesus Ministries

BAWUGI
15TH ANNIVERSARY EDITION
PRESS ON TO HIGHER GROUND
REV. RITA

Unless indicated otherwise, all Scripture quotations are taken from the Authorized King James Version of the Bible. Copyright © 1976 by Thomas Nelson Publishers, Inc.

From Milk To Meat A Compilation of Short Devotional Bible Studies To Guide Your Daily Walk With God.

Published by My All For Jesus Ministries, New Jersey, USA.

ISBN 978-1-61584-464-790000

Copyright © July 2009 by Rita Ann Bakr
All rights reserved

Author: Rita Ann Bakr
Editor: Marva Williams, London, U.K.
Cover design and photography: Rita Ann Bakr
Cover technical layout: Ben Knight
Printed in the United States of America

For it is God who makes all things possible

This Book is dedicated to the Glory and Majesty of God, who has given us His eternal inerrant Word to search out all matters.

To all who may read, may you be richly blessed, strengthened and guided as you seek to grow in God's Word, desiring it most sincerely, moving from milk to meat and living it to the fullest.

I acknowledge with deep gratitude and appreciation, my dear friend and sister in Christ, Marva Williams, for taking the time to edit this book.

CONTENTS.. **Page**

*I*ntroduction

From Milk to Meat is a compilation of weekly devotional Bible studies that I began writing and sharing with a wide reader audience some eighteen months ago.

It is truly amazing how God's Word is so in depth and captivating. As you study, you find that it requires much more than just a brief handling.

Some of the studies were initiated by my own experiences and convictions and as God's Word defines my life, they come directly from the heart.

From Milk to Meat is not just the title of this book, but also one of the devotional studies with the same name, which guide readers to strive to go deeper into the Word and search it out for deeper spiritual truths and direction and not just be contented with a simplistic understanding of the Scripture.

Moving from milk to meat is to be the desire of every Christian. Surely newborn babes desire the sincere milk of the Word that they may grow thereby, but after that must come the need for the meat of the Word to be a Spirit-filled, sustaining, life-changing, life-growing and fruit-bearing endeavor.

As you meditate on the contents of this book, may God through His Word grant you the desire to know, to grow and to be of full age ready for strong meat.

This book is to be read along with your Bible. All Scriptures are taken from the Authorized King James Version.

Humbly in Christ,

Rita

"Moreover it is required in stewards that a man be found faithful" (1 Corinthians 4:2). "For everyone that useth milk is unskillful in the word of righteousness: for he is a babe. But strong meat belongeth to them that are of full age . . ." (Hebrews 5:13, 14).

BACK TO THE BIBLE

Pick it up, dust it off, open it, pray, read it, meditate, and obey.

In times like these we need the Bible. We must read the Bible and pray every day. When we read God's Word we will encounter Him there with His presence, with truth and with the answers.

*T*HE INERRANT WORD OF GOD

"In the beginning was the Word, and the Word was with God, and the Word was God" (John 1:1)

I once heard someone who had grown up in the church and claimed to be a Christian, say that she found it hard to believe the Old Testament teachings which seemed to be folklore. I staggered with surprise and sadness at this blunt admission and was moved to share with her some Scripture about the inerrancy of God's Word. No doubt there are those who have a vague or little understanding of the Bible. Many others disdain its truths, seek to distort and discredit its teachings, live by a different authority and see the Scriptures through their natural eyes and, therefore, cannot comprehend its truths because "the natural man receives not the things of the Spirit of God: for they are foolishness unto him: neither can he know them, because they are spiritually discerned" (1 Corinthians 2:14).

God has given us His Word as the essence of Himself. In it, we have a complete encounter with His personality, thoughts, directives, commandments and teachings. If we are pleased to identify with Him, to claim His salvation and to accept His blessings, then we are to be pleased to accept His divine Word as accurate, true, infallible and inerrant. God is a God who cannot lie (Titus 1:2). He is from everlasting to everlasting (Psalm 90:2). He is holy and

10

supreme and we are to listen to His voice and live by every Word that proceeds out of His mouth (Matthew 4:4).

Scripture cannot be clearer when it proclaims the truth that "In the beginning was the Word, and the Word was with God, and the Word was God" (John 1:1). We learn from these Words that the Word is as old and durable as God Himself who gave it, and we have the confirmation of the Old Testament with the New Testament that "the grass withereth, the flower fadeth, but the Word of our God shall stand forever" (Isaiah 40:8). And "heaven and earth shall pass away but My Words shall not pass away" (Matthew 24:35). The Psalmist declares that God's Word is true from the beginning and forever settled in heaven and every one of God's righteous judgments endures forever (Psalm 119: 89, 160).

What makes God's Word inerrant? It is God who makes this to be so. He breathes it from His holy being and declares that "All Scripture is given by inspiration of God" and profits the recipients greatly (2 Timothy 3:16). He is governed by His own Word as we read in Psalm 138:2 "...For Thou (God) has magnified Thy Word above all Thy name." This precious Word is truth and it sanctifies (John 17:17; Ephesians 5:26) and is able to make us clean (John 15:3). It guides, for it is a lamp unto our feet and a light unto our path (Psalm 119:105), and it grows and multiplies (Acts 12:24), as it is spread throughout the earth. God declares that this same Word will judge us at the end. "He that rejecteth Me and receiveth not My Words hath one that judgeth him: The Word that I have spoken, the same shall judge him in the last day" (John 12:48). God's Word is not only inerrant, it is sacred and we are to honor and respect it in the way we receive it, believe it, obey it and teach it. We are not to be ashamed of the Word which is the Gospel of Christ: for it is the power of God unto salvation (Romans 1:16), and because God is in charge of His Word that goes out of His mouth, He declares that it will not return to Him void but will accomplish that which He pleases and it shall prosper where He sends it (Isaiah 55:11).

Why then are we not taking God's Word seriously? Why are we ignoring it or changing it to suit our fancies and defiling it and the Holy One who gave it, with our rebellion, disobedience and faithlessness? When we trash the Word, despise or reject it we are rejecting God who is the Word. And God warns us that those who despise His Word shall be destroyed, but those who fear His commandment shall be rewarded (Proverbs 13:13).

Let us endeavor to renew our interest in, and appreciation of God's Word and be under its authority. "So then faith cometh by hearing and hearing by the Word of God" (Romans 10:17). Let us be zealous to seek after it, to study to show ourselves approved unto God, a workman who is not ashamed of the Gospel, rightly dividing the Word of truth (2 Timothy 2:15). We must absorb it, precept upon precept, line upon line, here a little, there a little (Isaiah 28:13), compare spiritual with spiritual to understand and harmonize its teachings and our conclusions, and hide it in our hearts that we might not sin against God (Psalm 119:11). We must also give ourselves continually in prayer and the ministry of the Word (Acts 6:4). We can be like the Bereans who when they heard the Word, received it with all readiness of mind and searched the Scriptures daily whether those things were so (Acts 17:11). We can be like the prophets of old, who understood that the Word they received was indeed from God and held it in such awe and reverence, that it was hard to do anything less or more than it commanded. "I cannot go beyond the Word of the Lord my God, to do less or more" (Numbers 22:18).

The Old and New Testaments are both the Word of God and bear His indelible print on their pages, confirming and fulfilling the prophesies and teachings of each other. None of this is folklore, idle teaching, or words to dismiss. It is not man's words but God's, and in His divine wisdom and inerrancy makes this plain for all who would read and believe that we have a more sure word of prophecy; whereunto we will do well to take heed, knowing this first that no prophecy of the Scripture is of any private interpretation. For the prophecy came not in old time by the will of man: but holy men of God spoke as they were moved by the Holy Ghost (2 Peter 1:19-21). "The Lord gave the Word: great was the company that published it" (Psalm 68:11), and for this cause we are to thank God that when we receive it, we receive it not as the words of men, but as it is in truth, the Word of God, which effectually works also in them that believe (1 Thessalonians 2:13). When we make God's Word the

13

centerfold of our lives, we will find that it is enduring and able to do more for us than the words of man.

Jesus imparts God's Words to us and commands us to "Search the Scriptures for in them ye think you have eternal life; and they are they which testify of me (Jesus Christ)" (John 5:39). The Holy Spirit, who is the Spirit of truth witnesses to our spirits and guides us into all truth. He does not speak of himself, but glorifies the Father (John 16:13, 14). Our prayer should be like the Psalmist's "Open thou mine eyes that I might behold wondrous things out of thy law" (Psalm 119:18), and "Teach me O Lord, the way of Thy statutes; and I shall keep it unto the end. Give me understanding, and I shall keep Thy law; yea I shall observe it with my whole heart" (Psalm 119:33, 34). Let us not, therefore, depart from God, through a lack of understanding His Word and perish because of unbelief.

"Let the Word of Christ dwell in you richly in all wisdom; teaching and admonishing one another in Psalms and hymns and spiritual songs, singing with grace in your hearts to the Lord" (Colossians 3:16).

BE BLESSED TODAY AS YOU TAKE THE SWORD OF THE SPIRIT WHICH IS THE WORD OF GOD

*T*HE EXCELLENCY OF THE INERRANT WORD OF GOD

"In the beginning was the Word, and the Word was with God, and the Word was God" (John 1:1)

The Holy Scriptures are uniquely carved in God's own personality, it comes from Him, it is Him, it reveals His mind and He gives it to us as the guide for our lives. He is the sole author and authority of His Word and has inspired many scribes to write down His truths. No other word can compare to it. It is peaceable, convicting, trustworthy, without error and it is excellent. "Hear; for I (God) will speak of excellent things; and the opening of my lips shall be right things" (Proverbs 8:6). The Bible is its own interpreter (Genesis 40:8), it verifies itself (1 Corinthians 2:13), and there are no discrepancies or contradictions in the spiritual accounts of the scribes. There is absolute consistency in all its teachings.

Scripture tells us that those who are truly in Christ are filled with His Word, their lives are defined by it and they desire to affirm and obey its standards without challenge, argument or compromise. "But we have this treasure (the Gospel) in earthen vessels (ourselves), that the excellency of the power may be of God and not of us" (2 Corinthians 4:7). Believers are able to trust the Logos as the Word of truth and the Gospel of their salvation, ". . . in whom also after that ye believed, ye were sealed with that Holy Spirit of promise" (Ephesians 1:13). "For the Word was made flesh (Christ) and

15

dwelt among us . . ." (John 1:14). It is very near unto us, in our mouths and in our hearts that we may do it (Deuteronomy 30:14). It is not abstract, far removed or out of touch with our dispositions, and is a discerner of the thoughts and intents of the heart (Hebrews 4:12).

God's Word is spirit and life. Jesus told His disciples "It is the spirit that quickeneth; the flesh profiteth nothing: the Words that I speak unto you, they are spirit, and they are life" (John 6:63). It changes lives and we are admonished to seek after it. "Thy Word have I hid in my heart, that I might not sin against Thee" (Psalm 119:11). It is perfect, converting the soul; it is sure making wise the simple, it is pure, enlightening the eyes and right, rejoicing the heart and is to be desired than much fine gold (Psalm 19:7-10). The Word draws us to God and those who uphold its truths have no desire to depart from Him because He has the Words of eternal life (John 6:67).

The Word of God is also known as the Sword of the Spirit and it cuts to life or cuts to damnation because it is quick, and powerful, and sharper than any two-edged sword, piercing even to the dividing asunder of soul and spirit, and of the joints and marrow (Hebrews 4:12), and it will judge us at the last day (John 12:48). Moreover we are warned to heed it and promised that in keeping it there is great reward (Psalm 19:11).

There is no error in God's Word, it is sovereign and believers are to hang their whole life on it. The excellency of its very nature is seen in the power and authority it yields. It can take a dead soul and make it spiritually alive as we see in the Words Jesus spoke to Lazarus when he lay dead. "Lazarus, come forth" (John 11:43). And he did. (This is a picture of salvation that comes only through Jesus). There is no word of man that can command such power, truth, confidence and success. It can perform great miracles, "For whether is easier, to say, thy sins be forgiven thee, or to say, arise and walk?" And the man with the palsy arose and departed (Matthew 9:5-7).

The Word speaks of Jesus "And beginning at Moses and all the prophets, He (Jesus) expounded unto them in all the Scriptures the things concerning Himself" (Luke 24:27). It opens our understanding to the Scriptures (Luke 24:45), and as with the two men on the road to Emmaus, it opens spiritual eyes and burns hearts, "Did not our heart burn within us, while He talked with us by the way, and while He opened to us the Scriptures?" (Luke 24:30-32).

The excellency of God's inerrant Word is seen from where it comes and in what it does. "All Scripture is given by inspiration of God and is profitable for doctrine, for reproof, for correction, for instruction in righteousness: that the man of God may be perfect, throughly furnished unto all good works" (2 Timothy 3:16, 17). This means that God gives us His Word so that we are properly and truthfully scholared, and are rebuked and made aware of our sinful condition and our need of Jesus, our Savior. It corrects our focus from heading in the wrong direction and from any misguided comprehension of its teachings, and it instructs us in the ways of God, so that we are fully equipped to live for Him in all understanding and sincerity and to impart it to others. "Have not I written to thee excellent things in counsels and knowledge, that I might make thee know the certainty of the Words of truth; that thou might answer the Words of truth to them that send unto thee?" (Proverbs 22:20, 21).

We are to be thankful to God for giving us this excellent provision for our lives and we can say like the Psalmist, "My lips shall utter praise when Thou hast taught me Thy statutes. My tongue shall speak of Thy Word: for all Thy commandments are righteousness." (Psalm 119:171, 172).

"But the Word of the Lord endureth forever. And this is the Word which by the Gospel is preached unto you" (1 Peter 1:25).

BE BLESSED TODAY AND BE A DOER OF THE WORD NOT JUST A HEARER. ACCEPT IT, LIVE IT, SHARE IT

*J*ESUS SPOKE IN PARABLES

"... I will open My mouth in parables, I will utter what has been kept secret (hidden) from the foundation of the world" (Matthew 13:35)

The excellent inerrant and infallible Word of God is given to us in parabolic language. Most of the Bible is written in parables and this is a very important and crucial element in our understanding the Word of God. Scripture tells us that Jesus spoke in parables and without a parable He did not speak (Matthew 13:34).

A parable is an earthly story with a heavenly or spiritual meaning which is usually unspoken and implicit, and sometimes hidden from the hearer. It could be situational, historical or in the form of a story. Jesus was careful to teach in this language and give wisdom and hearing to those whom He would have to hear and understand. Why would Jesus teach in parables? He answers this in Isaiah 6:9-10 "And He (God) said, Go, and tell this people, Hear ye indeed, but understand not; and see ye indeed, but perceive not. Make the heart of this people fat, and make their ears heavy, and shut their eyes; lest they see with their eyes, and hear with their ears, and understand with their heart, and convert, and be healed." And similarly, in Matthew 13:13, "Therefore speak I to them in parables: because they seeing see not; and hearing they hear not, neither do they understand." This is so because "the preaching of the cross is to them that perish foolishness;

but unto us which are saved it is the power of God" (1 Corinthians 1:18).

Our header Scripture verse from Matthew 13:35, also found in Psalm 78:2, reminds us that eternal God was before the foundation of the world. One major work He did was to elect those whom He would save at that time (Ephesians 1:4, 5) and He manifests His salvation to fruition in their lives under the hearing and direction of His holy Word as He applies it to hearts. "So then faith cometh by hearing and hearing by the Word of God" (Romans 10:17), and ". . . as many as were ordained to eternal life believed" (Acts 13:48). Therefore, true believers everywhere are governed by God's Word, they must accept it as their sole spiritual authority and are to always obey it. No other word or doctrine must guide their lives and if they claim another authority besides God's, then the truth is not in them. God reveals His Word to His elect and they will sincerely hear it, believe it and seek to live by it while the non-elect will neither know nor understand God's Word and will merely pay lip service to its teachings. God considers them as having a form of godliness, but denying the power thereof and ever learning, and never able to come to the knowledge of the truth (see 2 Timothy 3:5 - 7).

We can admit that the Bible is not very easy to understand because much of it is written in parables and even Jesus' disciples who were close to Him did not always immediately grasp the meaning of what He spoke. Jesus knew this and took the time to explain to them because as His elect,

He was keen that they should know what He meant and not be ignorant of such things. On one such occasion after he had delivered the parable of the sower, Jesus asked them "Know ye not this parable? And how then will ye know all parables?" (Mark 4:13). He taught them His doctrine through parables as they were able to hear it. But without a parable He did not speak to them and when they were alone, He explained all things to His disciples. (See Mark 4:33, 34). They benefitted from His physical presence and teaching, we are to benefit from His written Word.

Jesus reminded them as He does us that "Unto you (the believers) it is given to know the mystery of the kingdom of God: but unto them that are without (the unbelievers) all these things are done in parables" (Mark 4:11). Those who are truly the children of God, will know the Master's voice. Jesus said "My sheep hear My voice and I know them, and they follow me" (John10:27), for they know His voice (John 10:4). God reveals His Word through the Holy Spirit which searches all things, yea, the deep things of God (1 Corinthians 2:10) and commands us to search the Scriptures for knowledge and understanding, for they (that is all the Scriptures) testify of Jesus (John 5:39). It is, therefore, wise, expedient and wholesome that we earnestly dig deep into the Scriptures and compare Spiritual with Spiritual, so as to fully understand and be conversant with the Word and bring forth its fruit in our lives. "It is the glory of God to conceal a thing: but the honor of Kings (the chosen) is to search out a matter" (Proverbs 25:2).

Parables are the primary method that Jesus used to teach about the kingdom of God (Matthew 13), salvation (Luke 16; John 3, 11), sin (Matthew 21; Mark 12; Luke 17, 20), (forgiveness (Matthew 18), commitment (Luke 14), false believers (Matthew 13; Mark 4; Luke 13), serving God (Matthew 25; Luke 19), fruitfulness (Luke 13), love (Luke 10), humility (Luke 14), persistence in prayer (Luke 11 and 18), the end times (Daniel 12; Matthew 13, 24, 25; Luke 12 and The Book of Revelation). This is by no means an exhaustive list - the entire Bible is - and so we must go to it with dedication, careful reading and meditation and pray for God's Holy Spirit wisdom and guidance to search out its hidden truths and make us overflow unto all riches of the full assurance of understanding the mystery of God the Father and of Christ in whom are hid all the treasures of wisdom and knowledge (Colossians 2:2, 3). What a tremendous blessing to those whom God is pleased to have ears to hear, eyes to see, hearts to receive and lives that glorify Him.

"The Lord God hath given me the tongue of the learned, that I should know how to speak a word in season to him that is weary: He wakeneth morning by morning, He wakeneth (opens) mine ear to hear as the learned" (Isaiah 50:4).

BE BLESSED TODAY AND REJOICE IN THE WISDOM AND UNDERSTANDING OF GOD'S WORD

TRIUNE MAJESTY

The majestic deity of God the Father, God the Son and God the Holy Ghost is glorified throughout the Bible and is to be so in our lives.

LEST WE FORGET

"Therefore shall ye lay up these My Words in your heart and in your soul . . ." (Deuteronomy 11:18)

Jesus came into the world for such a time as this. He was born to die. He was rich in His glory, knew no sin, but became poor as the Son of man, bearing enormous sin on the behalf of those whom He would save, in order that they could become rich with life everlasting. Such a rich man becoming a poor man for rich men is the story of salvation and one that has formed the basis of the Gospel and the purpose statement of the true child of God who believes that Jesus Christ is the Son of God; and that believing they might have life through His name (John 20:31).

As we celebrate the sacrifice of Jesus and the dusty road to the cross, we are celebrating God's divine purpose and plan to save fallen souls. His remedy for sin continues to be only through the atoning work of Jesus Christ, Savior of the world.

Lest we forget, according to the holy Scriptures, "And she shall bring forth a son, and thou shalt call His name JESUS: for He shall save **His** people from their sins" (Matthew 1:21); ". . . Christ died for our sins; and was buried and rose again the third day" (1 Corinthians 15:3, 4); "God commended His love toward us, in that while we were yet sinners, Christ died for us" (Romans 5:8); "For if, when we

were enemies, we were reconciled to God by the death of His
Son, much more, being reconciled, we shall be saved by His
life" (Romans 5:10); "For God so loved the world, that He
gave His only begotten Son, that whosoever (the saved)
believeth in Him should not perish, but have everlasting life"
(John 3:16); "So faith cometh by hearing, and hearing by the
Word of God" (Romans 10:17); "For the Son of man is come
to seek and to save that which was lost" (Luke 19:10); "All
that the Father (God) giveth me (Jesus) shall come to Me; and
him that cometh to Me I will in no wise cast out (John 6:37);
"No man can come to Me (Jesus) except the Father (God)
which hath sent Me draw him: and I will raise him up at the
last day" (John 6:44).

Lest we forget, the Scriptures remind us that all our
sins were placed on Jesus at Calvary when He bore the penalty
and curse of God on our behalf. We should not take it lightly
nor pride ourselves on a sacrifice well deserved. It is God's
indescribable gift of grace, not acquired by our own works of
righteousness. For it is by God's grace that we are saved
through Christ's faith; it is the gift of God, not of works lest
any man should boast (Ephesians 2:8, 9). "Neither is there
salvation in any other: for there is none other name under
heaven given among men, whereby we must be saved" (Acts
4:12). We can sing Hallelujah and praises to God even today
because of what Jesus did on our behalf.

"For He was wounded for our transgressions, He was bruised for our iniquities, the chastisement of our peace was upon Him and with His stripes we are healed" (Isaiah 53:5).

BE BLESSED TODAY AS YOU KEEP JESUS IN YOUR HEART

$\mathcal{H}$E IS RISEN

"Blessed be the God and Father of our Lord Jesus Christ, which according to His abundant mercy had begotten us again to a lively hope by the resurrection of Jesus Christ from the dead" (1 Peter 1:3)

Christ the Lord is Risen today[1]

Al---le---lu---ia

Sons of men and angels say

Al---le---lu---ia

Raise your joys and triumphs high

Al---le---lu---ia

Sing ye heavens and earth reply

Al---le---lu---ia

Christ is risen, risen in my heart today. He is risen in my mind, body and spirit.

He is risen in my prayer, my praise and my worship.

He is risen in my life of obedience to Him.

He is risen in the love I show you today, and in the debt that I forgive.

He is risen in the bread I share and the word I offer.

He is risen yes, He is risen indeed.

He is risen and is crowned with many crowns, the Lamb of God sitting on His throne, King of Kings and Lord of Lords.

He is risen and gloriously lives in me as I represent Him here on earth. His sacrifice is not in vain.

He is risen, He is alive and He knows about you and me. And because He lives, we too can live because God who raised Christ from the dead will also give life to our mortal bodies through His Spirit who dwells in us (Romans 8:11).

Is He risen for you today?

"I am crucified with Christ: nevertheless I live; yet not I, but Christ liveth in me: and the life which I now live in the flesh I live by the faith of the Son of God, who loved me, and gave Himself for me" (Galatians 2:20).

BE BLESSED TODAY IN THE GLORY OF THE CROSS AND THE NEWNESS OF LIFE WITH THE RESURRECTED CHRIST

$\mathcal{P}$RESERVED IN CHRIST

"Jude, the servant of Jesus Christ and brother of James, to them that are sanctified by God the Father, and preserved in Jesus Christ, and called" (Jude 1:1)

The words 'sanctified', 'preserved' and 'called' are referring to God's elect, His chosen ones before the foundation of the world (Ephesians 1:4), His saints whom Jesus died to save. And God does indeed preserve their salvation. Jesus confirms in John 17: 7-8 that all whom the Father has given Him have received His Words and know and believe in Him. Jesus has kept them and none are lost. In other words, they are safe in God's provision. Jesus also promises in Romans 8:35-39 that nothing will separate His elect from His love.

God is saying to His saints that they are preserved in Him and nothing will rob them of the gift of His eternal love and salvation. For once saved, they have a one-way access to the kingdom of heaven. They are sealed forever with the Holy Spirit of promise unto the praise of God's glory (Ephesians 1:13, 14). Philippians 1:6 and 2 Timothy 1.12 also testify of God's wonderful way of caring for and preserving His elect through the vicissitudes of life by performing His good work in them until the day of Jesus Christ's return. Psalm 121:7-9 assures that the Lord shall preserve His own from all evil. He shall preserve their soul and their going out and their coming in forever more.

One cannot deny that the world is filled with evil, doom and destruction. However, the believers while living in this environment are not at all isolated from its ills, but because they are preserved in Jesus Christ they are living in the abundance of His Word, understanding its truths and are guided to discern between good and evil and not be ensnared by false teachings and faulty doctrines. They are sustained so as not to fall prey to evil or be molded into the world's ways. They understand what behavior is acceptable and what is not in God's sight and their desire is to live in full obedience to God's will. In other words, they know the Master's voice and follow Him.

Those who are preserved in Christ, walk after the Spirit and not after the flesh (Romans 8:1 and Galatians 5:16). They keep themselves unspotted from the world (James 1:27) and gladly and truthfully share God's Word with others. They build themselves up in their most holy faith and pray as believers in the Holy Ghost (Jude 20). They keep themselves in the love of God, looking for the mercy of their Lord Jesus Christ unto eternal life (Jude 21), and by the great provision of the only wise God, they are kept from falling (Jude 24). Their salvation is secure, their lives are honorable; their walk is sure and undefiled and their faith is unshakeable. They are looking to, and trusting in God's ability, knowledge and wisdom to preserve them in a way they cannot do for themselves. For it is not by man's works of righteousness, that any should boast, but by God's grace that we are saved and preserved as salt and light, as peace and love, as children of God, redeemed, glorified and sanctified, looking away from this world and living in the blessed hope of Christ's imminent return.

"To the only wise God our Savior, be glory and majesty, dominion and power, both now and ever. Amen."
(Jude 25).

BE BLESSED TODAY PRESERVED IN CHRIST

$\mathcal{W}$ALKING IN THE SPIRIT

"This I say then, Walk in the Spirit, and ye shall not fulfill the lust of the flesh" (Galatians 5:16)

It seems that one of the hardest things to do is to walk in the Spirit, as the flesh is constantly at war with the Spirit. Satan has handed down the lie that no one is perfect and it is hard for anyone to be good, so why bother? Nothing is further from the truth. Scripture does tell us that no one is good and all have sinned and fallen short of God's glory (Psalm 14:1, Romans 3:10-12, 23). This is mankind's unsaved and unregenerate condition. However, Scripture also tells us that if any man be in Christ he/she is a new creature; old things are passed away, behold, all things have become new (2 Corinthians 5:17). We are also guided by these verses "Let this mind be in you which was also in Christ Jesus" (Philippians 2:5). ". . . But we have the mind of Christ" (1 Corinthians 2:16). These verses are of course referring to the new creatures in Christ; those who have been chosen to salvation through sanctification of the Spirit and belief of the truth and are indwelt by the blessed Holy Spirit. Galatians 5:16 is teaching us that those who are saved are able to please God, by walking in His indwelling Holy Spirit which sustains, guides, instructs, helps, illuminates, witnesses and fervently nudges the child of God out of the paths of the flesh and into the direction of Godliness and righteousness. "That which is born of the flesh is flesh; and that which is born of the Spirit is

32

spirit" (John 3:6).With men (in the flesh) this is impossible, but with God (in the Spirit) all things are possible (Matthew 19:26).

When we walk in the flesh, we are giving the devil a great foothold in our lives to direct and influence the desires of our heart and we know that from out of the heart come the issues of life, so when we walk in the flesh, the results are truly flesh-oriented, flesh-fulfilling, flesh-adulating and eternally destructive. "So then they that are in the flesh cannot please God" (Romans 8:8).

God tells us that the kingdom of God is not meat and drink; i.e. in eating and drinking and making merry (things of the flesh and of the world) but righteousness, and peace, and joy in the Holy Ghost, for he that in these things serves Christ is acceptable to God (Romans 14:17, 18). Therefore, as saved children we are empowered to walk in a new quality of life in the Spirit, and not fulfill the lust of the flesh, or give place to the devil, giving him the upper hand in our lives. We are reminded that he that sows to his flesh shall of the flesh reap corruption; but he that sows to the Spirit shall of the Spirit reap life everlasting (Galatians 6:8). So if we live in the Spirit, let us also walk in the Spirit (Galatians 5:25).

How do we then walk in the Spirit? Walking in the Spirit is Spirit-filled; it is not man-filled. There is no room for carnal thinking or acting, or for trying to balance a little bit of both. For if we invoke our own strength or power, we will fail and fall to the flesh and the spirit of the world. For to be carnally (flesh) minded is death; but to be spiritually minded is life and peace. For the carnal mind or the mind of the flesh is at enmity against God (Romans 8:6, 7), and the flesh profiteth nothing (John 6:63).

Walking in the Spirit means that we are saved and are living according to God in the Spirit who has established us in Christ and has anointed, sealed and given us the earnest of the Spirit in our hearts. We are, therefore, led of the Spirit which itself bears witness with our spirit that we are the children of God, and as children of God we follow God's rules. For as many as are led by the Spirit of God, they are the sons of God (Romans 8:14). It means that we show forth the fruit of the Spirit, which is love, joy, peace, longsuffering, gentleness, goodness, faith, meekness, temperance (Galatians 5:22, 23). It means that we are anointed with the unction of the Holy Spirit, we are transformed by the renewing of our minds, we have the mind of Christ and we know all things (Romans 12:2; 1 John 2:20, 27). It means that our desire is to do and be what God desires for us, having the Spirit of wisdom and we are built together for an habitation of God through the Spirit (Ephesians 2:22). In other words, God indwells us through His Holy Spirit and where the Spirit of the Lord is, there is liberty and freedom from sin and that which displeases God.

What a great way to begin each day by walking in the powerful Spirit of the Lord, being purposed, fervent and strengthened to serve in newness of the Spirit not in the oldness of the letter (Romans 7:6). It is expedient that we, therefore, watch and pray that we enter not into temptation: the spirit is willing but the flesh is weak. (Matthew 26:41).

"There is, therefore, now no condemnation to them which are in Christ Jesus who walk not after the flesh, but after the Spirit" (Romans 8:1).

BE BLESSED TODAY IN YOUR SPIRIT-FILLED WALK

$\mathcal{T}$HE WITNESS OF THE HOLY SPIRIT

"The Spirit itself beareth witness with our spirit, that we are the children of God" (Romans 8:16)

When Jesus was preparing to return to His Father in heaven, He promised His disciples to send the Comforter known as the Holy Spirit or Holy Ghost to be with them. It was expedient for them that He go away, for if He did not, the Comforter would not come (John 16:7). He had to leave them in order for the Holy Spirit to come and take up residence within their hearts, and not only them, but with all those whom He died to save.

The Holy Spirit who is the third person of the Blessed Trinity and who is the Spirit of truth, proceeds directly from God and testifies of Jesus Christ (John 15:26). He resides in the heart of all true believers and sustains them in their Christian walk. It is not by happenstance that we have this magnificent presence burning within us. It is all part of God's divine salvation plan that those whom He saved would be baptized (indwelt) by the Holy Spirit and not be left alone throughout their earthly pilgrimage and would be safely kept and spiritually sustained until Christ's return. The Holy Spirit convicts and reproves the world of sin and guides us in all truth. He does not speak of himself, but speaks of, and shows believers the ways of God. He glorifies God and imparts all Godliness and holiness to the believers (John 16:8, 13, 14). He teaches us what to say, giving us the words which we need and brings to our remembrance all that Jesus wants us to know (Luke 12:12; John 14:26).

As the Holy Spirit indwells us, He bears witness with our spirit, that we are indeed the children of God (Romans 8:16), and we know this. For as many as are led by the Spirit of God, they are the sons of God (Romans 8:14). His life and work is one of supreme authority, for the Spirit helps us in our infirmities and guides us in our prayer when we know not how to pray, making intercession for the saints according to the will of God with groanings which cannot be uttered (Romans 8:26, 27).

We bear Him about in us and display His precious fruit and are strongly cautioned not to blaspheme against Him (Luke 12:10) or allow impure thoughts, words and actions to grieve Hi blessed nature and quench His joy and promise with which we are sealed until the day of redemption (Christ's return) (Ephesians 4:30). We praise God for giving us a wonderful comforter, teacher, helper and friend.

"And when He (Jesus) hath said this, He breathed on them and said unto them, Receive ye the Holy Ghost" (John 20:22).

BE BLESSED TODAY AND BE LED BY THE SPIRIT

*T*HE LORD JEHOVAH

"The LORD whose name alone is JEHOVAH art the most high over all the earth" (Psalm 83:18)

THE LORD -

Formed man of the dust of the ground, and breathed into his nostrils the breath of life (Genesis 2:7).

Knoweth the way of the righteous (Psalm 1:6).

Is faithful, who shall strengthen you, and keep you from evil (2 Thessalonians 3:3).

Knoweth them that are His (2 Timothy 2:19).

Will bless His people with peace (Psalm 29:11).

Is gracious, and full of compassion; slow to anger and of great mercy (Psalm 145:8).

Is good to all: and His tender mercies are over all His works. (Psalm 145:9).

Is righteous in all His ways, and holy in all His works. (Psalm 145:17).

Is near unto them that are of a broken heart; and saveth such as be of a contrite spirit (Psalm 34:18).

Is not slack concerning His promise (2 Peter 3:9).

Redeemeth the soul of His servants: and none of them that trust in Him shall be desolate (Psalm 34:22).

The Lord is King for ever and ever (Psalm 10:16).

The Lord is worthy to be praised (2 Samuel 22:4).

Salvation belongs to the Lord (Psalm 3:8).

"I AM THE LORD YOUR GOD . . ." **(Numbers 15:41)**

THE LORD -

Is my Shepherd I shall not want (Psalm 23:1).

Is my light and my salvation, whom shall I fear (Psalm 27:1).

Is a shield for me; my glory, and the lifter up of mine head (Psalm 3:3).

Is my rock, and my fortress, and my deliverer. (Psalm 18:2).

Is the portion of mine inheritance and of my cup (Psalm 16:5).

Is my helper (Hebrew 13:6).

Will perfect that which concerneth me (Psalm 138:8).

Will deliver, preserve and will strengthen (Psalm 41:1-3).

Liveth; and blessed be my rock (Psalm 18:46).

I will love thee, O Lord, my strength. (Psalm 18:1).

I will praise the Lord according to His righteousness: and will sing praise to the name of the Lord most high (Psalm 7:17).

". . . THE LORD OUR RIGHTEOUSNESS" **(Jeremiah 23:6)**

Your God, He shall fight for you (Deuteronomy 3:22).

Shall be unto thee an everlasting light and thy God thy glory (Isaiah 60:19, 20).

Our God is in all things that we call upon him for (Deuteronomy 4:7).

The joy of the Lord is your strength (Nehemiah 8:10).

"I am the Lord: that is My name: and My glory will I not give to another, neither My praise to graven images" (Isaiah 42:8)

39

"... LET THE LORD BE MAGNIFIED" (Psalm 35:27)

Wait, I say, on the Lord (Psalm 27:14).

That all the people of the earth might know the hand of the Lord, that it is mighty: that ye might fear the Lord your God for ever (Joshua 4:24).

Serve the Lord with fear, and rejoice with trembling (Psalm 2:11).

Stand fast in the Lord (Philippians 4:1).

Rejoice in the Lord alway (Philippians 4:4).

Prepare the way of the Lord, make His paths straight (Matthew 3:3).

NOW MAY THE LORD OF PEACE HIMSELF GIVE YOU PEACE ALWAYS BY ALL MEANS AND THE GRACE OF OUR LORD JESUS CHRIST BE WITH YOU ALL. AMEN.

$\mathcal{T}$HE POWER TO WILL

"Teach me Thy way, O Lord; I will walk in Thy truth: unite my heart to fear Thy name" (Psalm 86:11)

God has set forth beautiful and enduring characteristics of Himself as eternal God, so that we may know that He is creator, faithful, trustworthy, dependable, available and able to deliver. We see in the Scriptures abundant evidence of His ability to do what He says and to do more than we can ever ask or imagine. His grace is sufficient, His wisdom is infinite, His ways are beyond understanding, His provision is unsurpassed and in Him is all power, majesty and the authority to do as He sovereignly wills. Here is what He confidently and truthfully declares of His ability. These are statements of fact and promise and Words to live by.

"Follow Me, and I **will** make you fishers of men" (Matthew 4:19).

" . . . Him that cometh to me, I **will** in no wise cast out" (John 6:37).

"Come unto me, all ye that labor and are heavy laden, and I **will** give you rest" (Matthew 11:28).

". . . I **will** never leave thee or forsake thee" (Hebrews 13:5).

". . . Be thou faithful unto death and I **will** give thee a crown of life" (Revelation 2:10).

When we submerge ourselves in the Scriptures and walk with God, we are never disappointed or left to wonder about His care and the fulfillment of His promises. We are amazed at His grace toward us, and the foundational truth, that we were saved by such a marvelous provision without any intervention or work of our own. God's I wills are the only way we can be saved and not through our works and they correspond to His divine plans.

The sovereignty and power of God the Father and the Son are revealed in some more I will pronouncements. For example, Jesus speaks to His elect, underscoring the importance of their obedience to Him as the only way of sincerely demonstrating their love to Him, and He guarantees His love as binding such a blessed relationship. He confirms "He that hath My commandments and keepeth them, he it is that loveth Me: and he that loveth Me shall be loved of My Father, and I **will** love him, and **will** manifest Myself to him" (John 14:21). He promises "And that whatsoever ye shall ask in My name that **will** I do, that the Father may be glorified in the Son (John 14:13), and repeats it by way of establishing its complete validity "If ye shall ask anything in My name, I **will** do it (John 14:14). "And it shall come to pass that before they call I **will** answer; and while they are yet speaking, I **will** hear" (Isaiah 65:24). He wills to deliver, preserve, strengthen, bless and save and since Scripture testifies that God does not lie (Romans 3:4), these 'I will' statements are words of fact guaranteed to impress upon us the nature of a true and sovereign God with divine power to accomplish what He sets forth. "Thou hast well seen: for I will hasten my Word to perform it" (Jeremiah 1:12). "God has not spoken in secret. I the Lord speak righteousness, I declare things that are right" (Isaiah 45:19).

For example, God says to all whom He has saved "I **will** give you a new heart and I **will** put My spirit within you and cause you to walk in My statutes ... and I **will** be your God" (Ezekiel 36:26-28). To those who are walking with Him, they have His assurances that He **will** extend peace like a river and comfort (Isaiah 66:12, 13), and those who have forsaken God, He promises "I **will** utter my judgments against them, touching all their wickedness . . ." (Jeremiah 1:16). To those whose walk is neither here nor there, whose faith and testimony are lukewarm, neither hot nor cold, God promises ". . . I **will** spue thee out of My mouth" (Revelation 3:16). This means He will have nothing to do with them.

We have a great opportunity, as it is still the day of salvation, to align ourselves with a loving, caring, trustworthy Father. We should be compelled to lay our lives on the line in humility, obedience and with the utmost desire to please Him. However, doing this on our own strength will only result in frustration and failure. We must pray and implore the gracious guiding of our Savior and Lord to infill us with His strength and will and prepare our hearts to affirm "Not my will but Thy will be done." Can we like the Psalmist desire to walk in ways that please God and include as our prayer and determination the following?

"I will praise Thee, O Lord, with my whole heart; I will show forth all Thy marvelous works. I will be glad and rejoice in Thee: I will sing praise to Thy name, O Thou most high" (Psalm 9:1, 2).

"I will bless the Lord at all times: His praise shall continually be in my mouth" (Psalm 34:1).

"I will sing of mercy and judgment: Unto Thee, O Lord, will I sing. I will behave myself wisely in a perfect way. . . I will walk within my house with a perfect heart. I will set no wicked thing before mine eyes: I hate the work of them that turn aside; it shall not cleave to me. A forward heart shall depart from me: I will not know a wicked person" (Psalm 101:1-4). With this wellspring of life we are confident that "in the day of my trouble I will call upon God, for He will answer me" (Psalm 86:7). We can boldly say "the Lord is my helper, and I will not fear what man shall do unto me" (Hebrews 13:6), and ". . . I will dwell in the house of the Lord forever" (Psalm 23:6).

"I will remember the works of the Lord. Surely, I will remember Thy wonders of old" (Psalm 77:11). ". . . I will give thanks unto Thee for ever" (Psalm 30:12).

BE BLESSED TODAY WITH POWER AND THE WILL TO SERVE GOD FAITHFULLY

$\mathcal{A}$LTOGETHER LOVELY

Looking beyond myself and into the wonderful face of my Savior, the warmth of His love melts my sorrows, cleanses my sins and rejuvenates my desire for Him.

My beloved Lord is altogether lovely.

GOD WILL TAKE CARE OF YOU

"Casting all your care upon Him for He careth for you"
(1 Peter 5:7)

I am moved to write these words with care, prayer and concern for some dear friends and all others who are waging a battle with the harshness of cancer and other health issues and for those under the weight of broken or failed marriages. In times like these when the burden is great, pain is extreme and disappointment and anguish prevails words may seem inadequate. However, it serves well to remember the Words and promises of our great and provisionary Almighty God, who knows of all suffering and who is able to do exceedingly more than we can ever ask or imagine. He Himself took our infirmities and bare our sicknesses. (Matthew 8: 17). Jesus reminds us that in this world we will have tribulation, but we are to fear not for He has overcome such. (John 16:33). All who hope in the Lord are to be of good courage and He shall strengthen your heart (Psalm 31:24). Though our outer man perish the inward man is renewed day by day (2 Corinthians 4:16), for every day lived in faith, love and closeness to Jesus feeds the spirit with His grace, peace and provision.

A dear hymn comes to mind which I lovingly share with reassurances that as you commit every care and concern, fear and tear to God, He will take care of you.

Be not dismayed whate'er betide[2]
God will take care of you
Beneath His wings of love abide
God will take care of you.

Through days of toil when heart doth fail
God will take care of you
When dangers fierce your path assail
God will take care of you.

All you may need He will provide
God will take care of you
Nothing you ask will be denied
God will take care of you.

No matter what may be the test
God will take care of you
Lean, weary one, upon His breast
God will take care of you.

God will take care of you

Through every day, o'er all the way

He will take care of you

God will take care of you.

**Wait on the Lord, be of good courage, and He shall
strengthen thine heart: wait, I say, on the Lord (Psalm
27:14).**

**JESUS IS A PRAYER AWAY, SEEK HIM, FIND HIM, CALL UPON
HIM, TRUST HIM AND BE BLESSED TODAY**

*L*OVE THAT NEVER FAILS

"Herein is love, not that we loved God, but that He loved us, and sent His Son to be the propitiation (covering) for our sins" (1 John 4:10)

The only reason mankind can love God or show any trace of love one for another is because the love of God is shed abroad in their hearts (Romans 5:5) and this is not filial or erotica love but agape God-breathed, unconditional love.

We are to be lost in wonder and awe and moved with great thanksgiving for such love that sets us free from sin. "For God so loved the world that He gave His only begotten Son, that whosoever believeth in Him should not perish, but have everlasting life" (John 3:16). The love that God shows to undeserving man is pure, enduring and perfected through Jesus Christ, and best of all it is His free gift. We can neither work nor do anything to earn it. Perhaps such realization moved the hymn writer to pen the words to the beautiful hymn, "Love divine all loves excelling, who from heaven to earth came down. Fix in us Thy humble dwelling; all Thy faithful mercies crown."[3]

Love that never fails hung at Calvary's cross, lay in the sepulchre and is now seated at God's right hand, and will one day return in spectacular glory as a bridegroom coming for His bride – all those who truly believe in and have lived for Him. Love that never fails was evident in Jesus' tender care for His disciples as He taught and shepherded them. It is

found in His teaching on the Sermon on the Mount, when He pronounced multiple blessings on the least in status (Matthew 5) and in His heartfelt prayer that God would protect His loved ones from the evil of judgment day (John 17:15).

Love that never fails is demonstrated in God's great promise that nothing will be able to separate the true believers from His love which is in Christ Jesus (Romans 8:39). Those who place their trust in God will find comfort and assurance in His priceless agape love which transcends all others, and never fails and on which they can rely. This is so because the Holy One offering it is Himself love (1 John 4:8) and is wise. He is faithful, does not lie (Romans 3:4) and is the same yesterday, and today and forever (Hebrews 13:8) and His Word is forever settled in heaven (Psalm 119:89).

And what about the recipients of this grace, can their love also never fail? How can they demonstrate this? Jesus provided the answer in His Words of John 14:15, 21. "If you love Me, keep My commandments. He that has My commandments, and keeps them, he it is that loves Me: and he that loves Me shall be loved of My Father, and I will love him, and will manifest Myself to him." It is by our obedience and sincere devotion to God, by loving Him with all our heart and soul and mind that we can exemplify our steadfast love to Him. This is not love that is equal to God's but love that responds to God's that also allows us to live in the unity of the Holy Spirit and to love our neighbor as we love ourselves. It causes us to pray for others and to encourage the weaker sibling, spouse, friend or co-worker and yes, even our enemy, in the things of the Lord because we desire their spiritual best as we seek ours.

And if we were to speak with great eloquence and be endowed with remarkable knowledge and credentials and fail in love, we have nothing (1 Corinthians 13:1-4).

"But whoso keeps God's Word in him truly is the love of God perfected . . ." (1 John 2:5).

GOD CREATED LOVE. GOD PERFECTS LOVE. GOD SUSTAINS LOVE. GOD IS LOVE

$\mathcal{H}$AVE MERCY

"Hear, O Lord, (when) I cry with my voice: have mercy upon me, and answer me" (Psalm 27:7)

Scripture records the cries of two blind men sitting by the way side. When they heard that Jesus was passing by, they beseeched Him with all their might "Have mercy on us, O Lord, Thou Son of David" (Matthew 20:30). Scripture also records the prayer of the publican, who had nothing in himself to offer God, but pure cries of "Lord, be merciful to me a sinner" (Luke 18:13).

Mercy is described as kindness, compassion and forgiveness which God graciously gives to us who are undeserving and which we can never repay. "Have mercy" is to be a necessary cry in our lives, as a response to our need for God's intervention and salvation. We are reminded that it is not by works of righteousness which we have done, but according to His (God) mercy He saved us (Titus 3:5). We have the mandate to call on God for His infinite mercy and the invitation to come boldly unto the throne of grace, that we may obtain same (Hebrews 4:16). And especially as we look at our affliction, our sin, our weaknesses, our feeble state and our need for God, these words of beseeching should pour from our hearts and roll off our lips as we stand needy and humbly before a most merciful, kind and saving God. When we cry out for mercy, we are asking God for His favor to not give us what we truly deserve. "He that covers his sins shall not prosper, but he who confesses and forsakes them will have God's mercy" (Proverbs 28:13).

The Psalmist prays to God continually to have mercy on him and hear his prayer (Psalm 4:1). He cries out for mercy because he is weak and his bones are vexed (Psalm 6:2); because he is in trouble and consumed with grief (Psalm 9:13; 31:9); desolate and afflicted (Psalm 25:16). David cried out for mercy for his sin and sought God's loving kindness and forgiveness to blot out his transgressions (Psalm 51:1). Crying out for God's mercy has everything to do with seeking His salvation and we can do so as often as it takes and God does have it in abundance and will show mercy upon his afflicted and those that wait for Him (Isaiah 30:18; 49:13; 54:8); and upon whom He wants because it is His absolute prerogative, "I will have mercy on whom I will and I will have compassion on whom I will" (Romans 9:15).

Many today are seeking mercy from each other, to forgive hurts, to appease pain, to heal wounds and to right wrongs. Those who have received God's mercy can likewise show mercy to others as Jesus commands us to (Matthew 18:33; Luke 11:4). It is a definite quality of the child of God to forgive others as God has forgiven them and to be merciful to others as God has to you. And as the Apostle Paul noted of his ministry, one birthed by God's mercy and having renounced his ways of transgression ". . . as we have received mercy, we faint not" (2 Corinthians 4:1). If we are walking with God we are to be filled with joy and thanksgiving at His promise that goodness and mercy shall follow us all the days of our lives (Psalm 23:6). For without it we are doomed.

"Behold we count them happy which endure …and have seen the end of the Lord; that the Lord is very pitiful and of tender mercy" (James 5:11).

BE BLESSED TODAY IN GOD'S MERCY

*T*HE EYES OF THE LORD

"For the eyes of the Lord are over the righteous, and His ears are open unto their prayers: but the face of the Lord is against them that do evil" (1 Peter 3:12)

God's eyes are everywhere. He faithfully sees and knows our substance and every intimate detail of our lives and there is nothing hid from Him (Psalm 139:15, 16). He is the all-seeing, omnipresent judge. "The Lord looketh from heaven; He beholdeth all the sons of men" (Psalm 33:13). "For His eyes are upon the ways of man, and He sees all his goings" (Job 34:21). He sees my ways and counts all my steps (Job 31:4). There is nothing hid from Him.

Psalm 121:4 instructs us that God neither slumbers nor sleeps; therefore, He is awake and is watching over us and all that concerns us. His eyes run to and fro throughout the whole earth to show Himself strong in the behalf of them whose heart is perfect toward Him (2 Chronicles 16:9 and Zechariah 4:10).

God's eyes never tire or rest, they are not discriminating, they are in every place, beholding the evil and the good (Proverbs 15:3), protecting and punishing and nothing or no one is hid from its range and His observation. For the ways of man are before the eyes of the Lord, and He pondereth all his goings. (Proverbs 5:21). He sees us individually and collectively and knows what rule we walk by. He warns us "Behold, the eyes of the Lord God are upon the

55

sinful kingdom and I will destroy it from of the face of the earth . . ." (Amos 9:8).

God's eyes are not only seeing, but they are operating on our behalf. They are not physical but spiritual, providing watchful care over His children. "The eyes of the Lord are upon the righteous, and His ears are open unto their cry" (Psalm 34:15). They preserve knowledge (Proverbs 22:12); they guide, perfectly laying out the paths we should take so we are not walking alone and unsure. "I will instruct thee and teach thee in the way which thou shalt go: I will guide thee with Mine eye" (Psalm 32:8), and they care for the land. Yes, the eyes of the Lord thy God are always upon it (the land), "from the beginning of the year even unto the end of the year" (Deuteronomy 11:12) and even for such a time as this, our God is in all things that we call upon him for (Deuteronomy 4:7). He is in charge and great is His faithfulness.

Since God's eyes are on us, therefore, our eyes are to be ever toward the Lord (Psalm 25:15). We are to lift our eyes to the hills (i.e. God) from where comes our help (Psalm 121:1) and turn our eyes upon Jesus and look full in His wonderful face, fixing our affections on things above. Our eyes are to wait on Him until He has mercy upon us (Psalm 123:2), and our eyes must be trained to behold and scrutinize His infallible Word, for without its vision, we perish (Proverbs 29:18). The prophet Isaiah's eyes saw the King, the Lord of Hosts in His glory and that encounter left him painfully aware of his sinful condition (Isaiah 6:5-7). As our eyes see the prophecy of God's Word unfolding, we will say the Lord be magnified (Malachi 1:5), for every eye will see Christ when He comes on the clouds of glory. (Revelation 1:7). This is the Lord's doing; and it will be marvelous in our eyes (Psalm 118:23 and Matthew 21:42). May our eyes not be blinded or be the type that do not see (Jeremiah 5:21) but be open to the magnificence and the truth of God's Word which will guide us safely through this time and into eternity. We are to ask God to open our eyes that we may behold wondrous things out of His law (Psalm 119:18) and maybe like Noah, we will find grace in the eyes of the Lord (Genesis 6:8).

"The Lord is in His Holy Temple, the Lord's throne is in heaven: His eyes behold, His eyelids try the children of men" (Psalm 11:4).

BE BLESSED TODAY UNDER GOD'S WATCHFUL EYE

SATISFIED WITH GOD

**"Blessed is the man whom Thou (God) chooses and causes
to approach unto Thee, that he may dwell in Thy courts:
we shall be satisfied with the goodness of Thy house, even
of Thy holy temple" (Psalm 65:4)**

The nature of mankind is to be somewhat dissatisfied
with life. They can be dissatisfied with themselves, with work,
with pay, friends, their marriage and even with the weather.
There is always something that can cause dissatisfaction. ". . .
The eyes of man are never satisfied" (Proverbs 27:20).

The Israelites wandering in the wilderness were
dissatisfied with God and murmured for more food and water.
God provided bountifully but their first response was
murmuring and dissatisfaction (Exodus 15:24), they spoke
against God and said, "can God furnish a table in the
wilderness? (Psalm 78:19).

When we stop to think of what we have, both
material and spiritual blessings through God's marvelous
provision, we will find that we have everything we need in
order to be thankful and satisfied. Being satisfied is not just
being pleased with the stuff we have acquired, but being
contented in what God has done on our behalf. Being satisfied
is not in our material possessions which will come and go but
in our spiritual bounty which is for ever more. ". . . A man's
life consists not in the abundance of the things which he
possesses" (Luke 12:15).

Are we satisfied with God and His provisions or are we looking to other gods to fulfill our yearnings? "The fear (reverence) of the Lord tendeth to life and he that has it shall abide satisfied; he shall not be visited with evil" (Proverbs 19:23). Are we satisfied with God's Word as He has written it, does our heart stand in awe of it, or are we seeking to add our own words? Do His teachings convict us of our sin and stir in us a deep desire for repentance and peaceful reconciliation with God? Are we satisfied with the grace, mercy and peace He offers through His Son, Jesus Christ, or are we looking for external attributes to bolster our faith experience? Being satisfied with God means that we have made Him our refuge and strength (Psalm 46:1). He is our soul provider and our expectation and we wait upon Him (Psalm 62:5). We acknowledge Him as our God (Psalm 63:1), we give thanks in all things (1 Thessalonians 5:18), we seek a deeper and lasting fellowship with Him and our hearts never tire of His ways. Being satisfied is a condition of the heart which in times of plenty or lack, sadness or joy will proclaim that "my soul shall be satisfied as with marrow and fatness (goodness); and my mouth shall praise thee with joyful lips" (Psalm 63:5).

God has established the earth and it abideth. He has given us life everlasting through His salvation. He is faithful and merciful. His promises are sure and never broken. Heaven and earth shall pass away but God's Words shall not pass away (Matthew 24:35). We have access to Him through prayer and the reading of His holy Word and He sheds His light on us every day so that we can abide contented in Him and in the excellence of His loving kindness. Therefore, all who put their trust under the shadow of His wings shall be abundantly satisfied with the fatness of His provision (Psalm 36:7, 8). We have the blessed assurance that He shall supply all our need according to His riches in glory by Christ Jesus (Philippians 4:19). He will perfect all that concerns us and will not forsake the work of His own hands (Psalm 138:8). He will guide us safely through eternity (John 10:28), and God expects His people to be satisfied with His goodness (Jeremiah 31:14 and 50:19). From whom else can we obtain salvation and such a sure Word of promise and hope? "For every good and perfect gift is from above, and cometh down from the Father of lights, with whom is no variableness or shadow of turning" (James 1:17).

Knowing what we know of God, and as we enjoy daily fellowship with Him, we are to praise Him and be satisfied with His provision, His promises, His wisdom, His work of salvation and His guarantee of eternity future. As we are fed each day with the bread of life by the Bread of Life, Jesus Christ, we are satisfied that we shall never hunger or thirst (John 6:35). The meek shall eat and be satisfied: they shall praise the Lord that seek Him . . . (Psalm 22:26).

I am satisfied with God. I trust you are. However, the question remains, is God satisfied with us? May we live in such a way, that He is not ashamed of us when He comes in glory (Mark 8:38) and will say "Well done thou good and faithful servant. . . Enter thou into the joy of thy Lord" (Matthew 25:21).

"As for me; I will behold thy face in righteousness: I shall be satisfied, when I awake, with Thy likeness" (Psalm 17:15).

BE BLESSED TODAY AND BE SATISFIED WITH ALL GOD OFFERS

*F*OR EVER AND EVER

". . . The kingdoms of this world are become the kingdoms of our Lord, and of His Christ; and He shall reign for ever and ever" (Revelation 11:15)

For unto us a child is born

Jesus Christ, a babe in a manger in Bethlehem

He grew up in Nazareth

Taught in the temples

Overturned tables

Healed the sick, gave sight to the blind

Comforted the mourning and gave strength to the weary.

Jesus Christ, born a babe in a manger in Bethlehem

Praying for the saints, casting out devils

Leading His disciples, standing up to the opposition.

Jesus Christ, born a babe in a manger in Bethlehem

Hanging on a cross, bearing my sin and yours

Pardoning the thief on His right

Bowing His head when His work was finished

Born to die.

Rising three days after

Appearing in full glory to His chosen

Returning to heaven and is seated on the right hand of God,

His Father

He is looking at you, looking at me

He is waiting, praying, helping, and interceding.

And in the fullness of time
He will return with the sound of the trumpet and the shout of
the angels
To reclaim His people, His elect, His beloved, His saved
All those who have faithfully occupied until His return
and rapture them to Himself
Where they shall reign with Him in peace for ever and ever.

Jesus Christ, born a babe in a manger in Bethlehem, died, was
resurrected, and is alive and well in my heart and yours and
holy is His name.

Jesus is heaven's eternal gift.

**". . . Alleluia: for the Lord God omnipotent reigneth. . .
King of Kings, and Lord of Lords" (Revelation 19:6, 16).**

BE BLESSED TODAY AND FOR EVER

*D*IVINE COMMANDS

When God speaks, we have no choice but to hear.
His Words are pure and penetrate our spirits. He
tells us that if we love Him we are to keep His
commandments and with His help we can.
We are His sheep and know His voice.

*G*o!

"Go ye therefore, and teach all nations . . ." (Matthew 28:19)

Jesus has given us an imperative to **GO** and do things in His Name. He sends us to minister to others, care for the sick, pray for the unbelieving, bear one another's burdens and teach and preach His Word, and He tells us to be as wise as serpents and harmless as doves (Matthew 10:16).

He guarantees that we would not be alone but would enjoy the blessing and comfort of His divine presence wherever we go and even when the going gets rough. The command to Go is as valid and timely today to true believers everywhere as it was when Jesus instructed His disciples to take off in His Name.

When we Go, we set out to accomplish much in Jesus' name and by His strength and guidance. God had a Word and a mission for those whom He sent. They were not going idly, they were going with specific directions to fulfill His mission and they were going in faith to achieve God-glorifying results. God commanded Noah and his family to "Go forth of the ark" (Genesis 8:16). This was specific to God's plan to save them from the flood. And they went.

God instructed Moses "Go to Pharaoh and say to him, thus saith the Lord, Let my people go, that they may serve me." This was an enormous assignment that Moses was undertaking in God's name to bring forth God's chosen people to the Promised Land. When they resorted to sinful habits of building and worshipping idols while Moses was meeting with God and receiving His law, God charged him to "Go, get thee down, for thy people have corrupted themselves" (Exodus 32:7). He sent Moses to intervene and restore order and Godliness in the camp.

Jesus sent His disciples to untie a colt and bring it to Him and to gather the necessities to prepare the Passover (Matthew 26:18; Mark 11:2, Mark 14:13). He gave them work to do and was teaching them obedience, responsibility and discipline which are core Christian values. He told the woman with the issue of blood to "Go in peace" because her faith had saved her (Luke 7:50). She departed from His presence healed and saved. The man who was blind from birth was sent to "Go, wash in the pool of Siloam" (John 9:7). He responded in faith and came away seeing. The leper was charged to tell no man of his encounter with Jesus but "Go and show himself to the priest" (Luke 5:14).

If our zeal for service is misplaced or done according to our own works designed to serve God and mammon, Jesus forbids such tendencies and guides us to get in step with His program. He told the rich young ruler who was seeking God and the kingdom of heaven on his own merits, that he lacked one thing, and charged him to Go his way and take care of it, sell what he had and give to the poor. (Mark 10:21). It was necessary for him to sever his ties to earthly treasures and then return and follow Jesus who wanted that nothing stand in the way of their relationship. He is teaching us that our works of righteousness are defective and do not put us in good standing with God. We are to take up the cross and follow Him. God told Saul to arise from the ground and "Go to Damascus" to receive his missionary and apostolic appointment (Acts 22:10). The Holy Spirit breathed this instruction to Philip "Go near, and join thyself to this chariot" (Acts 8:29). His assignment was specific and resolute, i.e. to boldly witness the Word of God to the Ethiopian Eunuch and baptize him. Saint John the Divine in His vision of the end times was instructed by a voice from heaven to "Go and take the little book which is open in the hand of the angel standing upon the sea and earth" (Revelation 10:8). These divine commands were not empty instructions, they were sure and enlightening the eyes (Psalm 19:8b), they did not return void but prospered in the thing whereto God sent it (Isaiah 55:11).

Not only are we instructed to Go and speak words of life, but we are to Go from the presence of that which is foolish and not bringing the true Gospel (Proverbs 14:7) and we are not to go hastily into contention with others (Proverbs 25:8). "How beautiful upon the mountains are the feet of him that brings good tidings and publishes peace . . ." (Isaiah 52:7). As Christ's disciples we are to stoop to receive His directives for service and are to faithfully execute them so that they conform to what He wants. We do not go aimlessly or self-opinioned, but prepared, being instant in season and out of season as we take the Word to others (2 Timothy 4:2). We are to work the work of Him who sent us while it is yet day. The night cometh when no man can work (John 9:4). Jesus said, "Behold I come quickly . . ." (Revelation 22:7) so before that happens, we are to Go out into the highways and as many as we find, we are to bid to the marriage (Matthew 22:9). God promises to never leave or forsake us and to be with us wherever we go, even to the end of the world (Matthew 28:20). The good news is that He does not just send us but comes along as well. Jesus said to His disciples as they boarded a ship to go to the other side of the lake, "Let us go" (Luke 8:22).

Jesus Himself was on divine assignment and promised His disciples "I Go to prepare a place for you . . . that where I am, there ye may be also" (John 14:2). He is showing by example that He takes His Father's work seriously and that He truly loves and cares about his saints enough to go to prepare their eternal habitation in heaven that at the divinely appointed time they will join Him there. He is also reassuring the true believers they are not to worry about their earthly existence as He promises a more glorious dwelling place in His Father's house.

"Stand therefore, having your loins girded with truth . . . and your feet shod with the preparation of the Gospel of peace" (Ephesians 6:14, 15).

BE BLESSED TODAY AND GO WHERE THE SAVIOR LEADS. GO IN FAITH AND WITH THANKSGIVING

DOING IT GOD'S WAY

"If ye love Me, keep My commandments" (John 14:15)

Sometimes we have difficulty conforming to the rules and authority of others. We are not always easily molded or reined into a different frame of mind or way of doing things. Ours is the tried, tested and proven way. We like it like that, why should we follow another methodology?

However, we have a higher and ultimate authority in God. He is all-wise, all-knowing and ever present. He knows everything about everyone and everything about everything. His methodology is supreme and His greatness is unsearchable. There is no shadow of turning or variableness in what He does (James 1:17).

God commands us to keep His commandments. He takes it a step further that would test our love for Him. For it is easy to say we love Him while living as though we do not. He does not hold us to lip service, fantasies or rituals but desires a deep heart-felt committed and obedient relationship with Him. He wants us to be not just hearers or readers of the Word but doers (James 1.22). He says if you love me, then prove it. Show me. ". . . Keep my commandments" (John 14:15). This is the greatest proof the true believer has to support their claim to being a child of God – that is, their obedience to Him, and it is translated, "Doing it God's Way". We can ask ourselves; do

I have a deep desire to obey God? Do I want to do things His way? Do I have a great reverence for His holy Word?

If the answer is yes, then the going gets easier. When we are confronted with decisions, choices, enticements or peer pressure and are forced to evaluate our choice of action, then we are to simply stop and do it God's way, for the fear of the Lord is the beginning of wisdom: a good understanding have all they that do His commandments (Psalm 111:10). When we follow God's rule and authority, the burden of making bad choices or decisions becomes much less. The results are God-honoring and we are kept at peace and in His will. "Great peace have they which love thy law: and nothing shall offend them" (Psalm 119:165).

For example, God has given us the Sunday Sabbath to be set aside as His holy day to worship and enjoy spiritual rest in Him, we must then keep it as such and turn away our feet from doing our own thing and make the Sabbath a delight (Isaiah 58:13). God forbids adultery, so we are to obey that teaching and not pursue such relationships. God tells us that what He has joined together in marriage, no man must put asunder (Mark 10:9) we are, therefore, to understand that divorce is not an option. When God says we are to seek Him first and His righteousness, then our response is to be Thy face Lord, will I seek and early as well (Psalm 27:8 and 63:1). God cautions us about worry and anxiety and promises His grace is sufficient for us and He will meet our every need. We are to then be good stewards of His blessings and be contented with such things as we have and embrace His assurances that He would never leave or forsake us (Hebrews 13:5), and that He will perfect all that concerns us (Psalm 138:8). God has given instruction to children to obey their parents in the Lord: for this is right and to honor father and mother. We do so unhesitatingly, because this great commandment with promise augurs well with those who obey. And when God instructs us to pray and faint not, we pray our way through the day with such prayers rising from sincere lips (Psalm 17:1).

When confronted with decisions and choices, if there is ever a doubt or uncertainty as to which road to go, tossing a coin is not the answer, nor are we to choose the high road of dishonorable solutions. Doing it God's way means we are committed to obeying someone higher than us, that we understand it is better to trust in the Lord than to put confidence in man (Psalm 118:8). We acknowledge and trust the Bible as His inerrant teaching and guiding Word which is pure and more to be desired than gold and by keeping of such there is great reward (Psalm 19:10, 11). This life is only temporal and our highest blessing will be fulfilled where God promises life everlasting for those who walk uprightly before Him.

Let us walk around in God's Word, seeking to know what He says. We should not be afraid to read and test His Word, rest in His promises and rely on His provision. And at the end of the day we can declare like the Psalmist, "My soul

has kept Thy testimonies; and I love them exceedingly"
(Psalm 119:167).

**"Teach me Thy way, O Lord, and lead me in a plain path .
. ." (Psalm 27:11).
"Give me understanding and I will keep thy law" (Psalm
119:34).**

BE BLESSED TODAY AND DO ALL GOD'S WAY

DON'T STRIKE THE ROCK

"And Moses lifted up his hand, and with his rod he smote the rock twice . . ." (Numbers 20:11)

In my human mind, one of the saddest events of Biblical history was when Moses forfeited the honor of leading the children of Israel into the promised land after all he had done on God's behalf. God had placed a special calling on Moses and his brother Aaron to confront and speak to the hardened Pharaoh and bring the children of Israel out of Egyptian bondage and shepherd them for forty years through the wilderness and eventually to the promised land of Canaan. God raised up Moses to show His power through him and for God's name to be declared throughout all the earth (Exodus 9:16). Scripture records of Moses, "There has never been another prophet like Moses, whom the Lord knew face to face" (Deuteronomy 34:10). Moses, therefore, walked with God, talked with God and had many profound personal and supernatural encounters with God among which were the burning bush experience at Mount Horeb and the receipt of the Ten Commandments and the rule of law on Mount Sinai.

He was the one that God chose to teach and lead the children of Israel in His holy ways and he did all that God commanded him to do up to the point when he enquired of God on their behalf for water to drink. God gave him a specific instruction to speak to the rock but in his frustration and anger with the murmuring and dissatisfied group of nomads, Moses struck the rock instead and this displeased God, who pronounced the penalty for his disobedience – neither he nor Aaron would be allowed to lead the Israelites into the promised land which God was giving them (Numbers 20:12).

No doubt God is using this episode to provide an enormous teaching illustration for those who would walk with Him. We are to always honor God. We are to take heed lest we fall (1Corinthians 10:12) and be sure that we walk in total obedience to God, trusting Him with all our heart and not leaning on our own understanding (Proverbs 3:5). We are to acknowledge without doubting, all what God says as being wisdom and truth, and faithfully prove the results as God-ordained. We are to be careful that in trying to be everything to all people, we do not become a castaway as the Apostle Paul warned (1 Corinthians 9:27). We should not run ahead of God with impatience and frustration, misplaced zeal or pride. We are to both hope and quietly wait for His salvation (Lamentations 3:26) for He has promised to perfect all that concerns His children (Psalm 138:8).

In our daily walk and shepherding of others, it is important that we always listen for, and to God's voice, first and foremost above any other. We may be tempted to rely on our own insights and experiences and those of others and be sadly led to the wrong decisions. We can be drained from our ministries which can often respond to the pleasures and demands of others and not glorify God. We may neglect to continually fortify and refresh ourselves with the truth and assurances of His Word and, therefore, miss His instructions and the opportunity to exalt Him in the presence of others.

We must be careful to meditate on God's Word, hide it in our hearts, seek Him in all things and most of all be obedient to His instructions and follow His rules of conduct. Instead of striking the rock like Moses did, we are to speak to the rock. For the rock is a picture of Jesus Christ. Scripture tells us that "He is my rock and my fortress . . ." (Psalm 18:2). "He is my rock and my salvation . . ." (Psalm 62:2). ". . . The Lord is upright: He is my rock and there is no unrighteousness in Him" (Psalm 92:15). Why then would I want to strike the rock? We are also to lean on the rock, because the eternal God is our refuge and underneath are the everlasting arms (Deuteronomy 33:27).

Moses was only allowed a glimpse of Canaan, the Promised Land from the distance of Jordan, but he did not set foot thereon. He did well in preparing the people for this triumph but he failed God in the last lap. As we meditate on this teaching from the Words of Scripture, let us therefore, run this race with God-sense and perseverance and pray to receive the full blessing of God and His crown of righteousness as we faithfully love and serve Him

"Take heed unto thyself, and unto the doctrine; continue in them: for in doing this thou shall both save thyself, and them that hear thee" (1 Timothy 4:16).

BE BLESSED TODAY AND STAND ON CHRIST THE SOLID ROCK

WAITING ON GOD

"Make haste, O God, to deliver me; make haste to help me, O Lord" (Psalm 70:1)

For many of us, waiting is a very hard thing to do. We are part of a society that desires instant results, instant gratification and instant answers. No matter where we are, whether in traffic, in supermarket lines, on the phone or in a waiting room, we find it unbearable to wait.

Even in our prayers to God, we ask Him to make haste to help us, especially when the answers are not forthcoming and it seems that we would have to wait. The result is that we become anxious, we intensify our prayers and we may even try to generate our own answers and forge results.

God has a word for those who are in a rush or are impatient. He exhorts them to **WAIT**. That's it. We are simply to wait on Him. ". . . Wait, I say on the Lord" (Psalm 27:14). He tells us in Isaiah 40:31 that those who wait on Him shall renew their strength. He recognizes that both young and old alike have the same tendency to be impatient and they are to wait on Him. He has a word to the young in the same Scripture, they shall run and not be weary; and to the old, He promises that they should walk and not faint (v31). While these seem to speak of a physical accomplishment, it goes beyond that to the spiritual, for those who are running and walking with the Gospel of Christ are promised the refreshment and strength they need to be effective Christians in their own walk and in their ministry as God uses His Word to guide their lives and all those who come under the hearing of it.

What are we waiting for? Is it for God to supply a present need, for an answer to a fervent prayer or for Christ's imminent return? Whatever the wait, we are commanded to use the time wisely and not give place to the devil or cave in to despair or hopelessness. We have to be careful to occupy during this waiting time, whether it be for a day, a year or more and trusting God for His answers, direction and revelation; using the time wisely, soberly, carefully and prayerfully. What do we do? We are to trust in the Lord with all our hearts, pour out our hearts to Him; acknowledge our sin, shortcomings and failings before Him; accept His chastisement if that's part of His answer; seek to do good; continue to do good, and the God of peace will keep our hearts and minds through Christ Jesus.

Are you waiting on salvation? God teaches that it is good that a man should hope and quietly wait on the salvation of the Lord (Lamentations 3:26). Psalm 123:2 says we are to wait on God until He has mercy on us. Are you waiting on the coming Christ? He says to "occupy till I come" (Luke 19:13) and to wait for His Son from heaven, whom He raised from the dead, even Jesus (1 Thessalonians 1:10). Are you waiting for healing physical or spiritual? God promises strength to the sick and binding up of that which was broken (Ezekiel 34:16).

Are you waiting for a change in your circumstances, whether it is for a job, a career change, a loved one to come to Christ or otherwise? Therefore, like Job, wait until your change comes (Job 14:14). Is the wait for a resolve to a long-standing conflict on the job, in the home or with family members? Rest in the Lord and wait patiently on Him to fight your battle. Psalm 37:9 promises that evildoers shall be cut off: but those who wait on the Lord, they shall inherit the earth. We are not to light our own fires and recompense evil for evil, but wait on the Lord and He shall save us (Proverbs 20:22). We are to acknowledge like the Psalmist "Because of His strength will I wait on Thee for God is my defense" (Psalm 59:9).

During our waiting seasons, we are to recognize that God is also doing a work in us and seeking to bring good into our lives, and what we wait for is far less important than what God is doing while we wait. He may be teaching us patience; He may be enlightening our eyes and our spirits to trust in Him only. He may be testing our faithfulness and He is certainly teaching us about his provisionary care which is not always as and when we expect but certainly according to His timing. We may have eyes for a particular answer, but in retrospect, we can admit, that our needs were met in better ways than we expected. For the Lord is able to do exceedingly abundantly above all that we ask or think (Ephesians 3:20). We are to appreciate His knowledge of our needs and His on-time provision and rejoice and be glad in Him (Psalm 9:2 and Psalm 70:4).

Waiting is tied to faith and expectancy that God will do something. God promises that those who wait on him shall not be ashamed (Isaiah 49:23). He is good unto them that wait for Him, to the soul that seeketh him (Lamentations 3:25). Therefore, let us ask God to lead us in His truth and teach us as we wait all the day on Him (Psalm 25:5) and may integrity and uprightness preserve us as we wait on Him (Psalm 25:21). Each of us can boldly say that my soul wait thou only upon God, for my expectation is from Him (Psalm 62:5).

"Wait on the Lord, be of good courage, and He shall strengthen thine heart: Wait, I say, on the Lord" (Psalm 27:14).

BE BLESSED TODAY AS YOU WAIT ON GOD. THE WAITING IS NOT IN VAIN

*B*EWARE OF THE LEAVEN OF THE PHARISEES

"And He (Jesus) charged them, saying, Take heed, beware of the leaven of the Pharisees, and of the leaven of Herod" (Mark 8:15)

When Jesus warned His disciples to be aware of the Leaven of the Pharisees and Herod, He was not speaking literally of bread and yeast but used the concept of the purpose of yeast which causes dough to rise to refer to the false doctrine of the Pharisees and Sadducees. He was speaking of hypocrisy (Luke12:1).

The Pharisees were the religious leaders of that day and were strict believers and adherers of the law. However, while they preached the strict rules of the law, they often times did not adhere to it themselves. That is why Jesus called them hypocrites (Luke 12:56). There were discrepancies in what they taught versus what they did and their shaky and hypocritical teachings were being espoused as truth. This is also pointed out in Matthew 23:2-3. Jesus warns us not to imitate, accept or follow the practices of the Pharisees and their false teachings. That means anyone who preaches, teaches or imparts the Word of God and behaves differently, not upholding it themselves. The hearing and doing teaching of James 1:23-25, is to be deeply rooted in our Christian walk and we are to stay focused on God's Word as our pillar.

The Leaven of Herod stemmed from the period of the Herods who basked in the praise of men, worldly lusts and inordinate power. Their ancestry was notorious for attacking the church, for killings and disposing of anyone who threatened their rule. This included attempts to kill the baby Jesus and the Apostle Peter and the actual killing of James, the Son of Zebedee. The Herods sought after the backing and support of the Jews on matters of mutual interest. Scripture tells us that Herod Agrippa so loved the praise of men that it became his downfall. He suffered death when he allowed men to call him god (Acts 12:21-23).

The leaven of Herod teaches us that we should not glory in the praise of man. All praise goes to God. It is heartfelt to be commended or recognized but we must be sure to give that glory to God who has blessed us with all our gifts. When Jesus referred to the Leaven of Herod, He was also teaching that we should be aware of those who try to destroy the Gospel, those who set themselves up as gods, seeking power, money, immorality and man's praise, who call evil good and good, evil and in that way diminish the real truth of the Gospel and, therefore, err from the faith. From such we are to turn away.

We see the Leaven of the Pharisees and Herod very much in evidence and prospering today with the preponderance of false teachings and followings, immoral lifestyles and the avid pursuit of temporal wealth which go against the Word of God. If we study to show ourselves approved unto God (2 Timothy 2:15), if we search the Scriptures for in them we find the true Gospel of Christ and have eternal life (John 5:39), if we try the Spirits whether they are of God (1 John 4:1), we will, therefore, not embrace or teach a false gospel. We must be careful to present the Gospel accurately as God's inerrant Word and not bow the knee to Baal (false gods). Our glorying in that which is not of God is an indication that our spiritual senses need to be sharpened with the truth. A little leaven leaveneth the whole lump (1 Corinthians 5:6). If it be bad leaven it is the same as one bad apple that spoils the whole barrel. Let us not grieve the Holy Spirit or give the enemy an occasion to blaspheme God.

Jesus said, "I am the Way, the Truth and the Life . . ." (John 14:6).

BE BLESSED TODAY IN THIS EXCELLENT WAY

BE NOT DECEIVED

"Be not deceived; God is not mocked: for whatsoever a man soweth that shall he also reap" (Galatians 6:7)

Deception is a worldly trait that raises its ugly head in many ways. We encounter it in relationships, in business, on the job and also in our spiritual walk. It is said that one can fool or deceive some of the people some of the time but not all of the people all of the time. And certainly there is one person whom we cannot deceive and that is God. Our Scripture text warns us about deceiving ourselves into thinking and behaving that we can pull one off on God or we can live contrary to His Word without Him noticing. God is not mocked. He sees and knows everything about us and our actions all have consequences. The above Scripture continues in verse 8 "For he that soweth to his flesh shall of the flesh reap corruption; but he that soweth to the Spirit shall of the Spirit reap life everlasting." Isn't it good of God to warn us of our own pitfalls and show us the rewards of living in His truths?

In the Old Testament days many people were determined to build and worship idols despite God's marvelous provision and His instruction through His prophets and commandments that they were not to have any other gods but Him. At every opportunity they got, they were seeking after other gods, and God warned them "Take heed to yourselves, that your heart be not deceived and ye turn aside, and serve other gods, and worship them" (Deuteronomy 11:16). God promised that His wrath would be kindled against them for such behavior and they would be deprived of His blessings (Deuteronomy 11:17).

King David committed the horrible sin of adultery in total disregard for his special relationship with God and the possible consequences which were quite severe as God levied punishment on him and his household (2 Samuel Chapters 11 and 12). The prophet Habakkuk was quite perturbed and burdened by the insipid sin which prevailed in his time. Good was overtaken by bad and bad flourished without restraint. He complained to God about the rampant iniquity of the wicked and the seeming lack of judgment from God. It was God's wisdom to remind him that He (God) was in control and His judgment was set for an appointed time and will come and not tarry. In other words, God would act in the fullness of His time. His silence was not to be mistaken as consent or being unaware (Habakkuk Chapters 1-4).

Ananias and Sapphira, the husband and wife team of Acts Chapter 5, who sold their belongings and then lied to the apostles about the proceedings from the sale, both met instant death for dealing treacherously with God. They were deceived into thinking that they could wittingly or unwittingly misrepresent the facts of the sale and lie to God and all will be well.

These examples all serve to teach us that we have to be totally honest in our dealings with God. He knows our down sitting and our uprising. He understands our thoughts from afar off. He is acquainted with all our ways and knows every word in our tongues (Psalm 139:2-4). We will certainly pierce ourselves through with many sorrows if we honor Him with our lips and have hearts that are far removed from obeying His Word. We need only to stop and consider our ways in the light of the repeated cautions and warnings we have from God that we are not to be deceived by our actions but we are to listen to, and believe in His Words. "Know ye not that the unrighteous shall not enter into the Kingdom of God? Be not deceived." And then God goes on to outline who He deems unrighteous (see 1 Corinthians 6:9). And we are to let no man deceive us about compromising our spirituality as Scripture is most clear on the nature of the righteous and the unrighteous (see 1 John 3:7-10).

There is no way that we can serve God without the authority of His Word and if we feel we can temper it to suit our needs, we are indeed deceiving ourselves. This also speaks to our wisdom and Scripture further cautions "Let no man deceive himself. If any among you seemeth wise in this world, let him become a fool, that he may be wise" (1 Corinthians 3:18). All that we do outside of God's commandments are nothing but deception. The truth is we are not deceiving God, but ourselves. ". . . The wicked is snared (trapped) in the work of his own hands" (Psalm 9:16). And this has devastating results.

In His end time teaching, Jesus elaborates to his audience on how He would view their self-righteousness and lack of love and care for the least in their midst. They were amazed at His stance toward their own self-deception. ". . . In as much as you did it not to one of the least of these, ye did it not to me. And these (the self-righteous) shall go away into everlasting punishment: but the righteous into life eternal" (Matthew 25:45, 46). The Bible is very clear about end-time deception, and reflects the mood of many who dismiss or downplay the fact that Christ will be returning (2 Peter 3:3-5), and from all accounts of Scripture, that day is fast approaching. Such deception tries to change the truth of God into a lie and this is indeed most dangerous for scoffers and those who are willingly ignorant of God's Word. Be not deceived, Christ will return and for many who are not expecting Him, He will come as a thief in the night and with all deceivableness of unrighteousness in them that perish; because they received not the love of the truth, that they might be saved (2 Thessalonians 2:10).

Finally, Jesus tells us to lay hold of sound doctrine which we get only through the faithful study of His Word, so that we are not deceived in these times by false teachers coming in His name and go after them (Luke 21:8). Our works will be tried in God's purifying fire and will stand on its own for what it is worth - hay, stubble, silver or gold.

"Let not him that is deceived trust in vanity: for vanity shall be his recompence" (Job 15:31).

BE BLESSED TODAY AND BE NOT DECEIVED: EVIL
COMMUNICATIONS CORRUPT GOOD MANNERS

Strictly Prohibited

"Wherefore let him that thinketh he standeth take heed lest he fall" (1 Corinthians 10:12)

From time to time we come across signs or notices that read 'strictly prohibited'. This means that wherever it is placed or whatever it speaks of is forbidden, banned, barred, illegal, outlawed or illicit.

If we are dare devils, impatient or non-observant, we may very well be inclined to ignore such signs and proceed to go against what it prohibits. Other signs may read 'caution', 'slow down', 'stop' 'keep off' or 'no entry' – all pointing to an act or area of activity that requires our attention and observance because if we do not, the results can be detrimental, catastrophic, negative, alarming, harmful and even fatal, either to ourselves or to others.

Scripture tells of an instruction that God gave to Adam and Eve as they enjoyed life fully in the Garden of Eden. They had free access to the Garden and its beauty except where God had set up His strictly prohibited sign in the midst thereof, in front of the tree of the knowledge of good and evil, and had warned them not to eat of it, for if they did, they would surely die. (Genesis 2:8-17). This warning, if ignored or broken had devastating physical and spiritual results. The penalty of death that God laid down referred to the eventual physical death of mankind and the spiritual death that ensued as a result of their disobedience. It was a falling away from God, a broken trust and a dismembered fellowship between God and His creation. "Wherefore, as by one man (Adam) sin entered into the world, and death by sin; and so death passed upon all men, for that all have sinned" (Romans 5:12). The results of breaking this strictly prohibited rule are exactly what God conveys in Romans 6:23 "The wages of sin is death."

King Saul did foolishly in the sight of God by not keeping His commandment or following His instruction to **wait seven days** for the prophet Samuel at Gilgal. He went ahead and forced himself against God's commandment and offered a burnt offering and thereby lost his kingdom (1 Samuel 13:1-14).

These grave violations of hard set rules prompted the question from God to Eve, "What is this thou hast done?" (Genesis 3:13), and from the Prophet Samuel to Saul, "What hast thou done?" (1 Samuel 13:11). Impatience, pride, self-reliance, arrogance, inconsideration and stupidity are all dispositions that can cause one to disobey or ignore imposed rules and restrictions and behave in a way that will prompt such an alarming question from God, from others and even from ourselves when we are faced with the consequences. And what may appear to be a simple or insignificant omission, oversight or act of defiance has deeper implications for the way we choose to view or not view God's rules for our lives.

As we ponder this, let us consciously keep our eyes open and our hearts and desires set to obey those signs God has placed in our way. They are given for a reason. The Bible is full of warnings that God lays down for our own good. He wants to stop us before we create a mess, wreak havoc, harm ourselves and others, destroy relationships, and particularly His and ours. He wants to avert the danger to our spirits from sin that so easily entangles us and prevent us from plunging headlong into spiritual destruction from which we may not recover. His strictly prohibited signs are not there to impose burly sanctions on us and deprive us from freedoms, but are there to guide and correct us, as well as foster harmony, obedience, peace and the understanding that our heavenly Father has set out guidelines and principles for us to live by and honor Him. And we are to use our liberty responsibly and not as a license to transgress or place a stumbling block in the path of others (1 Corinthians 8:9). God wants our undivided attention focused on His Words. He wants us to be careful and to pay attention. He tells us to "take heed".

For example, in speaking to Moses and the Hebrews, God gave them certain warnings, "And thou shalt set bounds unto the people round about, saying, Take heed to yourselves, that ye go not up into the mount, or touch the border of it: whosoever toucheth the mount shall be surely put to death" (Exodus 19:12).

"Take heed thyself, lest thou make a covenant with the inhabitants of the land whither thou goest, lest it be for a snare in the midst of thee" (Exodus 34:12).

"Take heed to yourselves, that your heart be not deceived, and ye turn aside, and serve other gods, and worship them; and then the Lord's wrath be kindled against you, and He shut up the heaven . . ." (Deuteronomy 11:16, 17). And these signs apply to us as well.

"Take heed, regard not iniquity . . ." (Job 36:21).

"Take heed to yourselves and bear no burden on the Sabbath day" (Jeremiah 17:21).

"Therefore take heed to your spirit, that ye deal not treacherously" (Malachi 2:16).

"Take heed that ye do not your alms before men, to be seen of them: otherwise ye have no reward of your Father which is in heaven" (Matthew 6:1).

"And take heed to yourselves, lest at any time your hearts be overcharged with surfeiting, and drunkenness, and cares of this life, and so that day (Christ's return) come upon you unawares" (Luke 31:24).

"Take heed, brethren, lest there be in any of you an evil heart of unbelief, in departing from the living God" (Hebrews 3:12).

Sometimes we may have to learn a hard lesson or two. But we are not to despise the chastening of the Lord or faint when we are rebuked of Him (Hebrews 12:5), but we are to be thankful that whom the Lord loves He chastens and scourges every son whom He receives (Hebrews 12:6). We are, therefore, to endure and purpose to be more diligent as we go along and take heed to our ways that we sin not.

". . . How then can I do this great wickedness, and sin against God?" (Genesis 39:9).

BE BLESSED TODAY, READ THE SIGNS AND OBEY

$\mathcal{A}$ TREASURED WALK

There is no better walk than the walk that pleases God. When we walk uprightly before God according to His Word, we are in step with His Will and the way that is life eternal. As our feet tread the paths to peace and righteousness, the gems we find there are priceless.

$\mathcal{F}$IVE A DAY FOR BETTER HEALTH

"O Taste and see that the Lord is good . . ." (Psalm 34:8)

I am sure this caption is a give away. It is one with which we are familiar. I actually took it from a very colorful, eye-catching pamphlet which listed the five servings of fruits and vegetables that one needs to consume each day for better health. Immediately, my mind transferred that into spiritual health. Good physical health is highly desirable, but physical health is no health at all without spiritual health. There is nothing wrong with eating healthy. We certainly ought to. However, let us also remember the invitation of Scripture to dine lavishly on God's goodness "O Taste and see that the Lord is good . . ." (Psalm 34:8).

Five a day Prescription for Better Spiritual Health is highly recommended.

> **Prayer**
> **Meditation**
> **Feeding on God's Word**
> **Praise**
> **Obeying God**

Let us not labor for the meat that perishes but for the meat that endures to everlasting life (John 6:27). That is for the healthy and hearty Word of the Gospel, that feeds, nourishes, gives life and sustains us to eternity (John 6:51, 58). In all that we get, let us get wisdom and strength from our Lord Jesus Christ. Let us be careful to seek after strong meat which belongs to them that are full of age, even those who by reason of use have their senses exercised to discern both good and evil (Hebrews 5:14). Let us also be careful to be not carried about by divers and strange doctrines. ". . . For it is a good thing that the heart be established with grace; not with meats which are unprofitable" (Hebrews 13:9). Knowing that man shall not live by bread alone, but by every Word that comes from the mouth of God (Matthew 4:4). "For the bread of God is He (Jesus) which cometh down from heaven, and giveth life unto the world" (John 6:33).

"And the Lord shall guide thee continually and satisfy thy soul in drought, and make fat thy bones: and thou shall be like a watered garden, and like a spring of water, whose waters fail not" (Isaiah 58:11).

BE BLESSED TODAY WITH SPIRITUAL HEALTH

𝓕AITH THAT PLEASES GOD

"But without faith it is impossible to please Him (God); for he that cometh to God must believe that He (God) is, and that He is a rewarder of them that diligently seek Him" (Hebrews 11:6)

Faith is a gift from God. It is not a feeling or emotion that we can give to ourselves or force ourselves to have. Those who believe wholeheartedly in God and His Word can do this on the premise that faith allows them to completely trust God at His Word, rest in Him, and know that although they do not have all the facts or answers for the present and the future they can risk the situation on Him, and be confident that whatever the outcome or result, it is part of God's perfectly ordained plan. The attitude of those who have faith that pleases God is evident in their abiding love for God, their trust, confidence and their security in Him and their patience in His sovereign work as He brings forth everything perfectly in its time. More than that, they have a joyful attitude, one that is filled with praise and thanksgiving for the gift of salvation that He has bestowed through His Son and filled them with faithful hearts which, although they cannot comprehend such magnanimous grace, thank God so much for it. The faith God speaks of is the faith of Jesus Christ which is a product of salvation and is evident in the life of the redeemed as the indwelling fruit of the Spirit (Galatians 5:22), and without such faith it is impossible to please God (Hebrews 11:6).

What is the size of our faith? Is it great or little? Is it like a grain of mustard seed of which Jesus spoke in His parable (Matthew 17:20)? Is it the type of faith that causes us to believe in God when everything around us seems bleak and many around us are skeptical or in unbelief? Can it make us whole? Can it move mountains because our will is aligned to God's will and our hearts are diligently seeking Him and our prayers are sincere? Are we nourished up in the words of faith and of good sound doctrine which we have attained (1 Timothy 4:6)? Can it stand in patience when tried (James 1:3)? The just shall live by this faith and if any draw back, God's soul shall have no pleasure in him.

"Let us therefore hold fast the profession of faith without wavering; for He (God) is faithful that promised" (Hebrews 10:23).

BE BLESSED TODAY WITH FAITH THAT CAN MOVE MOUNTAINS

*I*NVESTING IN ETERNITY

Are you looking for the ideal investment, where the yields are high, the home is prepared, the gas never runs out? Then read all about it in Matthew 6:33 and follow the instructions.

"Seek Ye First the Kingdom of God and His righteousness and everything else will be added"

When assets deflate, stocks wither and financial markets are in turbulence, investing in any portfolio is at best risky and those who are highly invested can be anxious and on edge. It seems that no amount of time, effort and planning can withstand the uncertainty and anxiety that follow disappointing returns.

However, there is a promised market where the dividends are paid up, the returns are guaranteed and the investment is well worth the time. This comes from investing in eternity where God's grace is free. We are to be concerned with investing in the assets of God's eternal kingdom which He has promised to all true believers. Luke 12:32 tells us that it is God's pleasure to give us His kingdom, and we can accept it without any fear of it being taken away from us. This is the great assurance that God gives those who put their trust in Him - something much greater and enduring than the things of the world. He promised that earthly riches will pass away, but His Word shall not (Matthew 24:35). He encourages us to seek His kingdom and His righteousness and not place our trust in uncertain riches (1 Timothy 6:17). He cautions us about serving God and mammon (money) as there is a great conflict of interest when one serves two masters. They will hate one and love the other (Matthew 6:24), and He reminds us that a man's life does not consist in the abundance of the things he possesses (Luke 21:4), and riches certainly make themselves wings and fly away as an eagle toward heaven (Proverbs 23:5).

By setting our sights on eternity we will also be living contentedly and sensibly without being excited and ensnared by the world's goods. "For what shall it profit a man if he gains the whole world and lose his own soul?" (Mark 8:36).While we can certainly enjoy our earthly blessings without turning them into idols, we can also pierce ourselves through with many sorrows from being covetous and worshipping them more than we worship God (1 Timothy 6:10).

It should not be difficult to set our affections on things above and build our hopes on things eternal, if we are carefully following Scripture and thinking of the glorious inheritance we have as children and heirs of God and joint-heirs with Christ (Romans 8:16,17). That is where our treasure is, and from all accounts of Scripture, where our treasure is, there will our hearts be also (Matthew 6:21).

Let us, therefore, follow sound advice and lay up in store for ourselves a good foundation against the time to come, that we may lay hold on eternal life whereunto we are called

(1 Timothy 6:19). This is done by being steadfast and faithful stewards, continuing in sound biblical doctrine and pressing toward the mark for the prize of the high calling of God in Christ Jesus (Philippians 3:14).

Those who are sincerely following Jesus' teaching will be guided and comforted by His blessing awarded to the poor in spirit (those who need God more than worldly possessions) - ". . . For theirs is the kingdom of Heaven" (Matthew 5:3). This is the eternal investment that we should be hastening toward.

"Labor not to be rich: cease from thine own wisdom"
(Proverbs 23:4).

BE BLESSED TODAY IN THE WONDERFUL BOUNTY OF GOD'S ETERNAL RICHES

Simply abiding

"Abide in me, and I in you . . ." (John 15:4)

Jesus teaches us the simple art of connecting to Him. He calls it abiding and John Chapter 15 shows us how. Here, Jesus instructs us to abide in Him and He will do the same in us. This invitation with instruction is filled with promise for those who would accept.

Abiding means closeness and relationship. As we abide in Christ and He in us, we are beneficiaries of an exclusive relationship with Him and God the Father, one that is saving and sustaining and highly rewarding. We see Jesus Christ as the true vine, and God the husbandman, able to make us clean through His Words (vv. 1, 3).

Abiding means permanency, rest and contentment. When Christ abides in us, and we in Him, we are sure to find stability as His Word and Spirit remain in us (1 John 2:24). "I have surely built thee an house to dwell in a settled place for thee to abide in for ever" (1 Kings 8:13). "He that dwells in the secret place of the most High (God) shall abide under the shadow of the Almighty" (Psalm 91:1).

Abiding means nurturing and bearing fruit. As branches attached to the vine (Jesus) we are nurtured, equipped and poised to bear fruit, and if we do not, God will purge and prune us in that direction (v. 2).

Abiding means abundant blessings. All who abide in Christ will bring forth much fruit, viz. the fruit of the spirit (Galatians 5:22), resplendent in a life lived out for Him, faith filled and discipled, winning souls for Christ (v. 8), joyfully bearing fruit in our old age (fat and flourishing) (Psalm 92:14), and glorifying God (v. 8).

Abiding means answered prayer. Connectivity to God, His Word and His will means we are to ask anything in His name and He promised it shall be done (v. 7). (1 John 5:14, 15).

Abiding is love at its best. "As the Father hath loved me, so have I loved you: continue ye in my love" (v. 9). We are instructed to keep God's commandments to abide in His love (v. 10).

We are not abiding with just anyone, but with the true vine and vinedresser Himself. This means that we are attached to Him, drawing from Him and feeding off of His strength, goodness and character. Because of this, in our abiding state, we can therefore, bring forth good fruit and do so abundantly in His name. Jesus expects this wonderful outcome of us, as He says, "I am the vine, ye are the branches: He that abideth in me, and I in him, the same bringeth forth much fruit: for without Me, ye can do nothing" (John 15:5). Do we have limitations to abiding and bearing fruit in abundance? Then let us search it out, confront it, pray about it and recommit ourselves to God. We desire to be fruitful and simply abiding.

"Let every man wherein he is called, therein abide with God" (1 Corinthians 7:24).

BE BLESSED TODAY AND ABIDE UNDER THE SHADOW OF THE ALMIGHTY

*W*HATSOEVER THINGS

"Finally brethren, whatsoever things are true, whatsoever things are honest, whatsoever things are just, whatsoever things are pure, whatsoever things are lovely, whatsoever things are of good report; if there be any virtue, and if there be any praise, think on these things" (Philippians 4:8)

In the Scripture above God provides a comprehensive list of honorable "things" that true believers are to be thinking on. This follows His most direct and reassuring Words of wisdom that tell us that we are not to be anxious or careful for nothing, not that we are to be lax or carefree, but in every thing by prayer and supplication with thanksgiving we are to let our requests be made known unto God (Philippians 4:6), whether it be for spiritual or material matters.

It is not uncommon for us to be concerned, anxious and worried over the complexities of life and if the truth be known, such worry and anxiety can all but consume our every thought. Our minds are filled and obsessed with details and possibilities and we can expend more thought than is needed on such matters. However, God in His great wisdom always provides guidance for us, so that we have the best opportunity to serve Him without distraction and the best outcome as His dear children to be at peace with Him and in Him through His saving grace, as Philippians 4:7 indicates "And the peace of God, which passeth all understanding, shall keep your hearts and minds through Christ Jesus."

We think with our mind and God wants to keep our thought process in harmony with Him and the pathway of our mind through Christ Jesus and He details the things we are to think on, viz. things that are honest, just, pure, lovely and of good report. These can be considered as the fruit of the mind of the true believer who is spiritually prepared to understand what God wants and is, therefore, in accord with the thoughts of Christ. Such thoughts as conveyed in His Word are to occupy our minds rather than godless images and thoughts unbecoming a person of faith. We are commanded to "let this mind be in you, which was also in Christ Jesus" (Philippians 2:5), and Scripture reinforces ". . . But we have the mind of Christ" (1 Corinthians 2:16). Not only do we have the mind of Christ but we are reminded that God has not given us the spirit of fear; but of power, and of love and of a sound mind (2 Timothy 1:7), and these gifts help us to withstand phony and belittling thoughts which do not rest on God's Word and deny His promises.

A closer look at the list of honorable whatsoever things on which we are to think will show that they are not in any way separate or different. They all speak of the same thing, i.e. God and His glorious Word. Whatsoever things are pure can be compared to Psalm 19:8 which declares that the commandment of the Lord is pure, enlightening the eyes. Whatsoever things are true refer to the judgments of the Lord, which are true and righteous altogether (Psalm 19:9); to God's Word which is true and forever settled in heaven (Psalm

119:89) and certainly to Christ Himself, who is the way, the truth and the life (John 14:6).

The converse of this is that if our minds are not in Christ Jesus, they are in the world and can become reprobate. This means God will allow behavior and actions that are in rebellion to Him to be unrestrained and follow the path of our minds (as a man thinks, so is he) and He will eventually leave us in that state of hopelessness (See Genesis 6:3 and Romans 1:28). Therefore, let us with fervent prayer and supplication set our affections on things above and bring into captivity every thought to the obedience of Christ (2 Corinthians 10:5), and love Him with all our heart, soul and mind (Matthew 22:37).

The beauty of all this is that God teaches that the honorable things listed above and His Word are to be desired more than much fine gold. So let us, therefore, think on these things.

"And be not conformed to this world: but be ye transformed by the renewing of your mind, that ye may prove what is that good, and acceptable, and perfect will of God" (Romans 12:2).

THINK ON THESE THINGS AND BE BLESSED TO ACT TODAY

WHERE IS MY FRUIT?

"But the fruit of the Spirit is love, joy, peace, longsuffering, gentleness, goodness, faith, meekness, temperance . . ." (Galatians 5:22, 23)

The believer who is indwelt by the Holy Spirit is filled with His fruit. Galatians 5:22 refers to them as 'the fruit of the spirit' and these are given to believers at the time of their rebirth. ". . . From me (God) is thy fruit found (Hosea 14:8)." They come as a total package, and hence the classification as 'fruit of the spirit.' They serve as our glorious inner core that exalts God whenever they are nurtured and exhibited. They are a testimony of God's handiwork and bless those who witness their outpouring. Maintaining this garden variety is hard work, especially if tended to by ourselves or are rarely in bloom. Our fruit must always be watered by the Word (Isaiah 58:11), weeded so as not to spring roots of bitterness that defile (Hebrews 12:15), pruned and cultivated by the vine dresser himself (God) (John 15:2), and blossomed into peaceable fruit of righteousness (Hebrews 12:11). They are certainly better than gold, yea than fine gold (Proverbs 8:19).

If not, they can be sown in weeds of insincerity, spiritual indiscipline, and sinful lifestyles that grieve and quench the Holy Spirit and thus become hidden, displaced and dried up, that we ourselves become wilted, lack-lustre

Christians who do not bloom or exude a fragrance that rises as a sweet smelling savor to God.

Am I angry – where is my fruit? Did I lie – where is my fruit? Is there covetousness in my spirit, pride in my walk, idolatry in my desires– where is my fruit? Did I utter unkind or harsh words – where is my fruit? Did I gossip, was I impatient, critical of others and seeking my own way, rather than God's - where is my fruit?

If we believe in God and exalt Him as Lord, we must, therefore, nurture our fruit with daily prayer and meditation and the studying of His Word, seek forgiveness always for any deviation there from, and enlist God's help to keep us pure and steadfast and then be careful to maintain good works, sanctifying the Lord God always in our hearts. And, therefore, "be as a tree planted by the waters, that spreadeth out her roots by the river, and shall not see when heat cometh, but her leaf shall be green; and shall not be careful in the year of drought, neither shall cease from yielding fruit" (Jeremiah 17:8).

Where is my fruit? It is in the hand of the Blessed Holy Spirit, planted deep within me, growing, blooming, and blessing. "For the fruit of the Spirit is in all goodness and righteousness and truth; proving what is acceptable unto the Lord" (Ephesians 5:9, 10).

"Herein is My father glorified, that ye bear much fruit, so shall ye be My disciples" (John 15:8).

BE BLESSED TODAY AND LET YOUR FRUIT BE ON DISPLAY

$\mathcal{M}$ARK THE PERFECT MAN

"Mark the perfect man (person), and behold the upright: for the end of that man is peace" (Psalm 37:37)

Many believers struggle with what it is to be perfect. They are either not sure if they are perfect or can aspire to perfection. Many hang on to the lie of the devil that they cannot be perfect and so relegate themselves to a faulty, mediocre or lack-lustre Christian existence, neglecting to move to higher ground because it seems so far out of reach or because they feel limited to what they can do and be as Christians. However, as we look into the Scriptures, we find many references to what God defines as perfect and this study seeks to share a few and clear up what might otherwise be a fear of, or disinterest in moving to, or seeking what God has provided to those who are in Him. We are to be guided by the amazing array of Scripture that teaches perfection from God's perspective.

1)   ". . . Noah was a just man and perfect in his generations, and Noah walked with God" (Genesis 6:9). To be perfect means we have to walk with God.

2)   God said to Abram, "I am the Almighty God; walk before Me, and be thou perfect" (Genesis 17:1). To be perfect means to walk uprightly before God, or stand sincerely before Him.

3)   In the Levitical laws, God described perfect sacrifices as having no blemish therein. To be perfect means to have no

blemish or impurities, giving God of the best, and that is of ourselves. We are called to present our bodies (ourselves) a living sacrifice, holy, acceptable unto God, understanding what is His good and acceptable and perfect will (Romans 12:1, 2). This is to be our reasonable service. To be perfect means to know and understand God's will for us, and we will find it all laid out in His Word. Without knowing and confirming to God's will we are imperfect, lost and living outside of His spiritual realm and His divine plans.

4)   "He (God) is the Rock, His work is perfect . . ." (Deuteronomy 32:4). We are the work of His hand, made in His image and likeness and we are perfect as He intended before sin changed our character. This is explained as being wonderfully and fearfully made in Psalm 139:14.

5)   "As for God, His way (Jesus) is perfect . . ." (2 Samuel 22:31). To be perfect means we are to seek after the perfect One, Jesus Christ, the way, the truth and the life.

6)   "Let your heart therefore be perfect with the Lord our God, to walk in His statutes, and to keep His commandments, as at this day" (1 Kings 8:61). This day means now, today. Our hearts are perfect when we are new creations in Christ. God says He will give us a new heart (Ezekiel 36:26-29) and the desire of our hearts must be to seek after and live for Him now, today and while we have time and breath. The Psalmist calls it 'early' (see Psalm 63:1).

7)   "Be ye therefore perfect, even as your Father which is in heaven is perfect" (Matthew 5:48). This is the achievable

imperative for us. Forget about what others say and trust what God says, i.e. we are to be perfect. He would never charge us with anything that He knew we could not accomplish in His name and through His grace. "I can do all things through Christ which strengthens me" (Philippians 4:13).

8)   "I (Jesus) in them, and Thou (God) in me, that they may be made perfect in one . . ." (John 17:23). This is taken from Jesus' heartfelt prayer to His Father for His disciples and His elect. He is acknowledging the source of all perfection which is in both God and Himself who are one and which are passed on to His elect who become one with them through the gift of salvation.

9)   Paul, through the divine inspiration of the Holy Spirit, exhorts us to be perfect, to be of good comfort and of one mind, to live in peace (2 Corinthians 13:11). This is the complete attitude of the true believer.

10)   "All scripture is given by inspiration of God, and is profitable for doctrine, for reproof, for correction, for instruction in righteousness: That the man of God may be perfect, throughly furnished unto all good works" (2 Timothy 3:16, 17). Our 'perfectness' aka perfection, comes from studying the Scriptures and obeying them and this is the hallmark of the Christian's life and the testimony of their completeness in Christ.

11)   "Now the God of peace . . . make you perfect in every good work to do His will . . ." (Hebrews 13:20, 21). Perfection comes from God. Only He is able to make us

perfect. It is His divine character and it is to be that of His children.

12)   "But let patience have her perfect work, that ye may be perfect and entire, wanting nothing" (James 1:4). This is the key to perfection – patience, and we are to be well disposed to the working of God within us to equip and sustain us in our entirety as a new creation in Christ, outfitted and complete in Him.

13)   Perfection is a perfect gift coming from above (James 1:17). Yes, it is a great gift from God and one that we should covet and strive for.

Scripture gives us the description of a perfect walk, and also about the unperfected. Lest there be any doubt, an imperfect heart is one that dwells in sin. "And he walked in all the sins of His father, which he had done before him: and his heart was **not perfect** with the Lord his God, as the heart of David his father" (1 Kings 15:3). This is referring to Abijam, David's grandson. There was also Amaziah who was Joash's son, who did not serve God with a perfect heart (see 2 Chronicles 25:2). Note in this account he did that which was right in the sight of the Lord, but not with a perfect heart. This teaches that we can be operating on the periphery by doing just enough Christian-looking or Christian-sounding things to get by but not really serving God with a perfect heart. God describes such as having a form of godliness, but denying the power thereof (2 Timothy 3:5). God wants all of our hearts and He must be Lord and ruler over all. We must be careful to harmonize our Christian walk with what God teaches in the Bible. Those teachings were valid then and are still most valid and trustworthy today. Jesus is talking to the church at Sardis, "Be watchful, and strengthen the things which remain, that are ready to die: for I have not found thy works perfect before God" (Revelation 3:2). He is also talking to many persons today who are serving two or more masters, and it will not work. It is to be 'God or' not 'God and'.

Scripture also highlights those who served God with a perfect heart, e.g. David (1 Kings 11:4), Asa (1 Kings 15:14 and 2 Chronicles 15:17), Hezekiah (2 Kings 20:3), Solomon started off well but his heart was perfect for a time only. He fell prey to evil and entertaining the sins of his many wives and did not walk fully after God (see 1 Chronicles 28:9; 29:19 and 1 Kings 11).

Is being perfect easy? Certainly not, and especially not by our own merits. It is to be cultivated with the promises of God, the Word of God and the strength of God given to us when we are reborn as a new creation in Christ fully equipped with the tools of the Spirit and a new direction and focus. It is sustained by knowing God's will and doing it. It is not a virtue, strength or disposition we acquire or can manipulate of our own. God makes us equipped, contained and confirmed to His desire for us. In this light, and in view of supporting Scripture, we are equipped for perfection. We must, therefore, prayerfully seek after and walk in that way. The end result of such a walk is peace, the kind of peace that will keep our hearts and minds through Christ Jesus. We are to be thankful for this encouragement and for these beautiful Words of Scripture "Great peace have they which love God's law: and nothing shall offend them" (Psalm 119:165).

"Let us therefore, as many as be perfect, be thus minded: and if in any thing ye be otherwise minded, God shall reveal even this unto you" (Philippians 3:15).

BE BLESSED TODAY AS A PERFECT CHILD OF GOD

*D*EW DROPS OF WISDOM

When wisdom enters the heart discretion shall preserve you, understanding shall keep you and your life will uphold and reflect what your heart and mind know to be so.

Wisdom from above

"But the wisdom that is from above is first pure, then peaceable, gentle, and easy to be entreated, full of mercy and good fruits, without partiality, and without hypocrisy" (James 3:17)

"The fear of the Lord is the beginning of wisdom: and the knowledge of the holy is understanding" (Proverbs 9:10). We are instructed to get wisdom, get understanding and not forget, decline or forsake her (Proverbs 4:5, 6). God sets out wisdom as the principal thing that we are to get and love, and when we do so we will also get understanding. This does not refer to the wisdom of the world, "for it is written, I (God) will destroy the wisdom of the wise, and will bring to nothing the understanding of the prudent" (1 Corinthians 1:19) because God has made foolish the wisdom of this world (1 Corinthians 1:20). The wisdom of the world is foolishness in the sight of God and detrimental to mankind because the world's wisdom is relegated to the lust of the eyes, the lust of the flesh and the pride of life (1 John 2:16).

Wisdom from above refers to Jesus Christ, the all-wise, all-knowing Savior, who imparts Himself to us and instructs and teaches us in the way we should go. And once wisdom enters into our hearts, we will be preserved and delivered from the way of the evil and forward man (Proverbs 2:12). Christ tells us to search the Scriptures for they testify fully of Him (John 5:39), and we will obtain wisdom,

117

knowledge and understanding that surpasses that of man and which direct us to eternal life. Wisdom that is from above will guide us into all things because it is first pure, that means it comes from God in whom are hid all the treasures of wisdom and knowledge (Colossians 2:3). It is peaceable, because it reflects the very nature of God, and its companion is discernment. It is gentle, because it does not seek to flaunt itself, be proud or promote strife, and it is easy to be entreated, because Jesus has given us the invitation to seek and ask in His name. He says ". . . Get wisdom; and with all thy getting get understanding" (Proverbs 4:7). Wisdom is the principal thing and it is full of mercy and good fruits, because it is of Christ and bears His mark and is evidenced in the character of the wonderful fruit of the spirit - love, joy, peace, longsuffering, gentleness, goodness, faith, meekness and temperance, which are all imparted to, and beautifully adorns the life of the child of God. It is without partiality - that means, it is no respecter of persons, and it is not obtained by pedigree, riches or education. It is there for all who will ask, and it is without hypocrisy, that means the offer is trustworthy and the assurances attached thereto are valid and enduring.

When wisdom enters our hearts, we have the tools, the teaching, the preparation and the foundation to live unto God and to glory in His presence. So we are to seek after it. It is better than rubies and all the things that may be desired are not to be compared to it (Proverbs 8:11).

As we reflect on this priceless and outstanding quality, which King Solomon chose above all else and which pleased God (1 Kings 3:9, 10), we must not forget that it has its beginnings in the fear (obedience) and understanding of the Lord and we are to truly desire it, and like the Psalmist, ask God **"So teach us to number our days, that we may apply our hearts unto wisdom" (Psalm 90:12).**

BE BLESSED TODAY AS YOU READ PROVERBS CHAPTER 4 FOR AN IN DEPTH TEACHING ON THE FATHER'S INSTRUCTION ON WISDOM

$\mathcal{T}$HE WISE MASTER BUILDER

"For other foundation can no man lay than that is laid, which is Jesus Christ" (1 Corinthians 3:11)

You have started a project, it is year two and it is still not done, despite your projections for completion. What is hindering it? What went wrong?

You think you are saved, but your life does not evidence this, you feel unfulfilled, uncertain and unenthusiastic about your witness.

Decisions! Decisions! Decisions! Which ones to make, what to choose, whom to see, where to go, how much to spend, what to offer God?

These are all common to us and as we ponder the path we should take with respect to our daily life and most of all our spirituality, let us be guided by some insightful and trustworthy verses of Scripture:

"Except the Lord build the house, they labor in vain that build it: except the Lord keep the city, the watchman waketh but in vain" (Psalm 127:1).

"Blessed is every one that feareth the Lord; that walketh in His (God's) ways" (Psalm 128:1).

"For we have this treasure (the Gospel) in earthen vessels (ourselves), that the excellency of the power may be of God, and not of us" (2 Corinthians 4:7).

"Not that we are sufficient of ourselves to think anything as of ourselves; but our sufficiency is of God" (2 Corinthians 3:5).

". . . The foolish man built his house on the sand . . . and the floods came, and the winds blew, and beat upon that house; and it fell, and great was the fall" (Matthew 7:26, 27).

"But they that wait on the Lord, shall renew their strength . . ." (Isaiah 40:31).

So whatever you desire to accomplish in the days to come, whether for things that are pending or the new challenges that arise and as you seek to grow in grace and closer to God, commit your way and your plans fully to the Lord's purpose and seek His will and He shall give you the desires of your heart (Psalm 37:5).

The wise master builder plans, prays, seeks God, prioritizes tasks, evaluates, prays more, depends on God, delegates when and where necessary, and thanks God always.

"Trust in the Lord with all thine heart and lean not unto thine own understanding. In all thy ways acknowledge Him, and He shall direct thy path. Be not wise in thine own eyes: fear the Lord, and depart from evil" (Proverbs 3:5-7).

BE BLESSED TODAY AS A WISE SERVANT AND AS YOU GET THE JOB DONE

121

*O*UR HIGH CALLING

"But ye are a chosen generation, a royal priesthood, an holy nation, a peculiar people; that ye should shew forth the praises of Him who hath called you out of darkness into His marvelous light" (1 Peter 2:9)

There are days when we may not particularly feel that we are good for anything. Folk may ridicule us, problems beset us, burdens weigh us down and we may even grow tired of our own selves, not feeling appreciated, loved, accepted by others or scorned and rebuffed when we try to share God's Word with those who are not interested or with those who have a different gospel.

While the flesh may feel this way our spirit ought to take heed of God's Word that encourages the destiny of the true believer with insight into who they are in Christ and how God views His elect. Those who are in Christ are chosen by God and are elevated to His higher calling. They must see themselves more than just living in the ordinary as earthly citizens but rather as living for the extraordinary as eternal citizens with sovereign guidance from God who propels them to shine His light in this dark world and to move beyond weakness, weariness, fear and uncertainty.

We are not to take our eyes off of Christ and place them on temporary distractions but are to seize the strength and assurances that God gives us in His Word and focus on being effective pilgrims, satisfied with who we are called to be. God guides His children with Scripture that emphasize their pedigree as chosen, royal, holy and peculiar (1 Peter 2:9). It means we are partakers of His heavenly calling with Jesus Christ as Apostle and High Priest of our profession (Hebrews 3:1), and we are fully endowed to bear God's royal mark and equipped to do His work.

Scripture also defines those who have God's high calling as ". . . lively stones, built up as a spiritual house, an holy priesthood, to offer up spiritual sacrifices, acceptable to God by Jesus Christ" (1 Peter 2:5), and being one body in Christ (Romans 12:5). We are led by the Spirit of God and are the sons of God (Romans 8:14), and if there be any doubt as to who we are in Christ, the Holy Spirit will bear witness with our spirit that we are the children of God (Romans 8:16). And this does not stop here, for if we are children of God, then our legacy is also in Christ Jesus as heirs of God and joint-heirs with Christ (Romans 8:17). This means true believers are individually and collectively beneficiaries of God's grace and share-holders in His eternal riches.

Our high calling in God is not based on pleasant sounding words that boost downtrodden egos, but on God's grace which lifts us up and draws us to Himself as a special people, vessels of mercy, saved, justified and glorified to live in accordance with His teachings and the fellowship of the Father, Son and Holy Spirit. For that we are known of God, we are no longer to desire to live as in the past when the truth was not in us and we were under the yoke of sin and in the fellowship of unrighteousness, but as God has called us from darkness into His marvelous light, we are to rise to that calling and show forth His praises to all without fear of rebuke or dismissal.

This is a beautiful truth which should help us live up to the challenges of any given day, as we make our calling and election sure and by our good fidelity demonstrate that we are a special workmanship because of who we truly are in Christ Jesus and with thanksgiving to God, "according as His divine power has given unto us all things that pertain unto life and godliness, through the knowledge of Him that hath called us to glory and virtue" (2 Peter 1:3).

"I press toward the mark for the prize of the high calling of God in Christ Jesus" (Philippians 3:14).

BE BLESSED TODAY IN THIS MARVELOUS ELEVATION

*I*DLENESS

"Now them that are such we command and exhort by our Lord Jesus Christ, that with quietness they work, and eat their own bread." (2 Thessalonians 3:12)

It is indeed wonderful that God in His great wisdom, knows the heart of all men and we cannot hide our thoughts or intents from Him. Because of this, God is well able, in His Word, to address all our character flaws. Yes, even idleness. The book of Proverbs speaks to the subject of idleness indicating that such souls shall suffer hunger (Proverbs 19:15), and the Apostle Paul under the inspiration of the Holy Spirit addresses this subject to the Thessalonians as some of them were found to be wanton in this regard. Some so-called believers of that day were misguided in their new found Christianity and did not quite understand the full implication of the teaching on Christ's return. They thought that they were saved, sanctified and were to sit idly by waiting to go to heaven, perhaps even continuing in sin and being disorderly. The truth of the matter is that, that attitude prevails in our midst today.

What are we saved for? The Gospel of Luke chapter 19 and verse 13 through parabolic reference admonishes believers to occupy until Jesus comes. We may ask occupy doing what? We are tasked to evangelize, spread the Gospel and tell others of Christ, to live for Him in word, deed and truth and be an ambassador for Him in our corner of the world.

Some Thessalonians did not understand this and were just sitting around, slothfully in self-indulgence and self-pity. Idleness can be a method the enemy uses to retard our spiritual walk, corrupt our witness and stagnate our ministry. It is a form of a false gospel that gives the wrong impression as to what our mandate on earth is to be as Christians awaiting Christ's glorious return. Idleness places the weaker person at a disadvantage and their motivation for Christ can be misplaced. It turns a would-be flourishing Christian into a distracted, intimidated, lack-lustre and defeated personality, who could easily revert to old unsaved habits and lapse in their faith, spiritual edification and commitment with their hearts turned from Christ.

Being idle in the ministry is just as bad as being a busybody in the ministry, living irresponsibly, running the wrong race and focusing our energies on activities that are not in harmony with God's will. Being idle not only relates to what we do but also to what we say and extends to how we use our words. Matthew 12:36 warns that every idle word that men shall speak, they shall give account thereof in the Day of Judgment. Therefore, we must be careful not to err in this manner and not learn to be idle, wandering about from house to house; and not only idle, but tattlers also and busybodies, speaking things which we ought not (1 Timothy 5:13).

Proverbs 31:27 calls us to take care of our household (that is ourselves and the places and persons where we have influence), and not eat the bread of idleness, i.e. anything that would feed and strengthen such a disposition. We should not give the devil a place in our lives or let the enemy prevent us from obeying God and furthering His kingdom here on earth. We are to use God's time wisely, laboring and working with our hands the thing which is good (Ephesians 4:28), and occupy and witness while we wait for Christ's imminent return. We have work to do and Scripture reminds us that we must work the works of Him (Jesus) that sent us while it is yet day for the night cometh when no man can work (John 9:4). How are we using our time and energy for God today? We are to see then that we walk circumspectly, not as fools, but as wise, redeeming the time, because the days are evil (Ephesians 5:15, 16).

"Wherefore, beloved, seeing that ye look for such things, be diligent that ye may be found of Him (Jesus) in peace, without spot, and blameless" (2 Peter 3:14).

BE BLESSED TODAY AS YOU MAKE FULL PROOF OF YOUR MINISTRY

*F*EEDING OUR ENEMIES

"Therefore if thine enemy hunger, feed him; if he thirst, give him drink: for in so doing thou shalt heap coals of fire on his head" (Romans 12:20)

I came across a quotation by Winston Churchill which reads "You have enemies? Good. That means you stood for something, sometime in your life." I thought of this in light of the witness of the true believers who undoubtedly encounter harsh and critical reviling and persecution from those who are opposed to the Gospel either in its full counsel or in a limited edition and are in essence the enemies of the cross.

The Bible gives many references to enemies, on a personal, national and spiritual level and outlines their activities and what they are capable of doing. For example, the Psalmist laments "Mine enemies reproach me all the day; and they that are mad against me are sworn against me" (Psalm 102:8). "Mine enemies speak evil of me, when shall he die and his name perish" (Psalm 41:5). "Mine enemies speak against me; and they that lay wait for my soul take counsel together" (Psalm 71:10). "Mine enemies would daily swallow me up: for they be many that fight against me . . ." (Psalm 56:2). The leaders and people of Israel encountered many enemies from neighboring nations and within their ranks (see Numbers 10:9; Deuteronomy 20:1; Joshua 10:13; 1 Samuel 4:3 and 20:16). The Psalmist called for God's enemies to be scattered (Psalm 68:1). The Apostle Paul under the inspiration of the Holy

Spirit cautions about pretense and having a superficial walk with God and describes those who denounce the true Gospel and follow their own as being the enemies of the cross of Christ (Philippians 3:18).

We are usually mad or disappointed with our enemies and seek either to avoid or confront them. However, God does not encourage us to get mad, get even, or to be an enemy of another person. He gives us a prescription to deal with our enemies, whether they are the ones in our own home (Micah 7:6), or enemies of the cross of Christ. God says, ". . . Love your enemies, bless them that curse you, do good to them that hate you, and pray for them which despitefully use you, and persecute you" (Matthew 5:44); we are even to lend to them, hoping for nothing in return (Luke 6:35). This seems to be a very unrealistic and difficult approach, for we would rather fight the enemy, prove ourselves better and right, and do our best to get even. To this disposition, God reserves reprisal as His prerogative. ". . . Vengeance is mine, I will repay says the Lord" (Romans 12:19). ". . . The Lord revengeth, and is furious; the Lord will take vengeance on His adversaries, and He reserveth wrath for His enemies" (Nahum 1:2). Scripture records that Balak's anger was aroused toward Balaam whom he co-opted to curse his enemies, but instead Balaam, under God's direction, blessed them three times (Numbers 24:10).

The worst work of the enemy is not so much directed to us by way of personal vendetta, petty jealousies or hatred, but in the persecution of the saints of God and opposing and frustrating the Gospel and the preaching of the cross. The Psalmist knew this very well and found it hard to encourage their friendship. He expressed hatred and grief toward those who spoke evil against God (Psalm 139:19-22).

Our enemies are hungry, they need God's Word. They are thirsty, they need spiritual drink and God equips us to feed them. Instead of avenging ourselves we are to side step wrath and ignite them with the Gospel. "Therefore if thine enemy hunger, feed him; if he thirst, give him drink: for in so doing thou shalt heap coals of fire on his head . . ." (Proverbs 25: 21-22 and Romans 12:20). This does not refer to physical food and drink, but the spiritual food found in the Word which we are compelled to share whether directly or implore through prayer. God is able to penetrate their consciences like burning coals of fire and draw them to Himself. God's touch is signified by the burning coals (see also Isaiah 6:1-9). We are not to fret ourselves because of the work of evildoers but pray for them and not against them (Psalm 17:8-14). We are to cease from all anger and forsake wrath (Psalm 37:1, 8). We are not to rejoice when our enemies stumble, lest the Lord see it, and it displeases Him, and He turn away His wrath from him (Proverbs 24:17-19). God shall reward us when we show genuine concern for the spiritual deliverance of the enemy (Proverbs 25:22).

God is well able to use the enemy for His purposes and turn their work around. They may initiate certain actions for bad, but God can formulate a good outcome, like He did with Joseph at the hand of his brothers who sold him to slavery (Genesis 50:20). God will scatter the enemy with His strong arm (Psalm 89:10). He will redeem us from the enemies for His mercy endures forever (Psalm 136:24) and God through His commandments will make us wiser than the enemy (Psalm 119:98). "When I cry unto Thee, then shall my enemies turn back: this I know: for God is for me" (Psalm 56:9). God will enable His children to chase their enemies who will fall before them by the sword (Leviticus 26: 7, 8). The word sword is used as a representation of the Word of God which is quick and powerful ... and is a discerner of the thoughts and intents of the heart (Hebrews 4:12). We are to call upon God who will save us from our enemies (Psalm 18:1) and believe with all our heart that when our ways please the Lord, He will make even our enemies to be at peace with us (Proverbs 16:7).

"Thou preparest a table before me in the presence of mine enemies, thou anointest my head with oil, my cup runneth over" (Psalm 23:5).

BE BLESSED TODAY AND BE NOT OVERCOME OF EVIL, BUT OVERCOME EVIL WITH GOOD

WHEN THE NEWS IS BAD

"He shall not be afraid of evil tidings: his heart is fixed trusting in the Lord" (Psalm 112:7)

The phone rings, there is news of the sudden death of a loved one or your child is in trouble. A job you were expecting fell through or you were overlooked for a promotion. The bank denied your loan application. The results of your medical test returned positive. Your health has taken a turn for the worse. The project you worked so hard on turned out to be a failure. Have you ever received bad news? What do you do?

Bad news is not selective and we can all be the recipients of it at one time or another. How we handle it is the key. God sets out many allegories in the Scriptures to teach us how to deal with bad news. For example, Hezekiah was sick unto death and the Lord sent Word to him through His prophet that he must set his house in order for he shall die and not live. To Hezekiah this was bad news. However, he did not roll over and die. He wept, prayed and recounted his faithful life to God and beseeched Him for mercy and God granted him healing and added 15 more years to his life (2 Kings 20:1 - 6).

Job was an upright and perfect man before God. He was enjoying a great life and fellowship with God and suddenly received devastating news that his children were all killed. He himself was struck with boils and great personal loss and suffering. This was bad news. However, in no way did Job despair, blame or curse God. He continued faithfully in prayer and communion with God and declared "though He slay me, yet will I trust in Him" (Job 13:15). He was confident that the Lord gave and it was His prerogative to take. ". . . the Lord gave and the Lord hath taken away; blessed be the name of the Lord" (Job 1:21).

God sent Jonah to warn the people of Nineveh about their wickedness and His plan to destroy them within 40 days. (Jonah 1 and 3:1-4). This was bad news for them. However, the people of Nineveh did not dismiss this ominous warning. They believed what God said, proclaimed a fast and repented and God saw their works that they turned from their evil ways and He changed His mind of the evil He said He would do unto them (Jonah 3:5-10).

God was displeased at the violence and corruption upon the earth and said "My Spirit shall not always strive with man" (Genesis 6:3). Noah then received bad news from God who purposed to destroy the world at that time by a great flood. Noah listened to God, and followed His instructions to build the ark and he and his family were saved. All others were destroyed. (Genesis 6:7, 13 and Genesis 7:1-24).

The Apostle Peter was told by Jesus that he would deny him three times. (Luke 22:34). He did not take it seriously as he felt that such a thing was impossible for he was a disciple and follower of Jesus and loved Him and could in no way deny Him. However, very soon after, when confronted with Jesus' arrest and possibly his own as well, Peter denied

Christ. The crowing rooster brought this startling prediction to his remembrance and he went out and wept bitterly (Luke 22:60-62). Bad news indeed.

Jesus bore in His spirit the bad news about mankind's sinful condition, with hearts that God pronounced to be deceitful and desperately wicked above all things (Jeremiah 17:9), and dead in trespasses and sins (Ephesians 2:1). However, God provided the cure and punished the curse of sin by sending His Son Jesus to be the propitiation for our sin (1 John 4:10), so that those whom He would save would be reborn to everlasting life. (John 3:16 and 10:27, 28). The bad news is that wherefore, as by one man (Adam) sin entered into the world, and (spiritual) death came about by sin; and so death passed upon all men, for that all have sinned (Romans 5:12). The good news is "But not as the offence, so also is the free gift. For if through the offence of one many be dead, much more the grace of God, and the gift by grace, which is by one man, Jesus Christ, hath abounded unto many" (Romans 5:15).

Bad news is not always the result of something we may or may not have done. Job said "I was not in safety, neither had I rest, neither was I quiet; yet trouble came" (Job 3:26). Bad news is not always God's punishment as some may think. And if it is, we are to embrace it. "For whom the Lord loves, He chastens and scourges every son whom He receives" (Hebrews 12:6). "Behold, happy is the man whom God corrects: therefore despise not thou the chastening of the Almighty" (Job 5:17).

When news is bad and even gets worse and life seems dark and dreary, empty and cruel, we are to look for good to follow. Sometimes news has to be bad before it gets good. And during those seasons that we are most affected, instead of responding in anger, self-pity, revenge, anxiety or self-loss, we are to take stock, reorder our thoughts and our focus and even change our direction and seek to learn what God is teaching us. We are to be willing and ready to confess our sins, repent of any underlying faults and sin not (Job 1:22). When the news is bad, we should not dwell on it more than we need to. We are to remember that God is ever with us with grace and power to see us through. We are to be prayerful and encouraged that good news shall eventually prevail. We are to hold on till our change comes (Job 14:14). While weeping may endure for a night (season) joy comes in the morning (Psalm 30:5). We are to read God's Word and there find strength, peace and courage to cope and we are to cry unto God most high, who performs all things for us (Psalm 57:2).

"What time I'm afraid, I will trust Thee (God)" (Psalm 56:3).

BE BLESSED TODAY. PRAY ALWAYS AND HOLD ON TO THE GOOD NEWS OF THE GOSPEL

*H*ow to sleep

**"I will both lay me down in peace, and sleep: for Thou,
Lord, only make me dwell in safety" (Psalm 4:8)**

When I was a child, I said this prayer before I slept
"This night when I lie down to sleep, I give Thee, Lord, my
soul to keep. If I should die before I wake please make me
good for Jesus' sake." As I grew older, my grandmother
taught me this prayer, "Jesus tender Shepherd hear me, bless
Thy little lamb tonight. Through the darkness be Thou near
me. Keep me safe till morning light." I am sure these have
also been the prayers of many little ones. Some may still be
repeating these words even to this day. These prayers provide
comfort for many little and grown hearts when they lay down
to sleep.

When I encountered Psalm 4:8, our Scripture verse, I
was immediately drawn to the testimony of a man (King
David), whose day was unpredictable and filled with a variety
of events that caused him much concern, alarm and even fear.
For example, his life was threatened by his adversaries, he was
challenged, he fought battles, he was a fugitive and hid in
caves. He dealt with rebellious sons and was himself subject to
temptation and great sin. And in all of these tribulations and
encounters, he knew of a great fellowship with God. Scripture
tells us that he was a man after God's heart (Acts 13:22), and
when he stumbled he was not utterly cast down (Psalm 37:24).
No matter how rough his day was, he was always in touch

with God and he knew how to lie down and sleep. He cried unto God and God healed him. God brought his soul from the grave and kept him alive (Psalm 30:2, 3). He did not take his cares to bed with him, but meditated on God's Word in the night watches (Psalm 63:6). He knew that great peace have they which love God's law: and nothing shall offend them (Psalm 119:165). He even rose at midnight to give thanks to God for His righteous judgments (Psalm 119:62), and God was His song in the night (Psalm 42:8).

What of us? We may not have such a day as David but we each bear our own share of challenges, trials, anguish, weariness and sickness that at times may threaten how we sleep at night. However, if we know enough of our provisionary and caring God, if our hearts are at peace with, and in Him, if we trust in His promises and take seriously His instruction that we are not to be anxious or worry about anything, but in everything with prayer and with thanksgiving we are to make our requests known unto God, we then have the blessing of His peace that surpasses all human understanding that will keep our hearts and minds through Christ Jesus (Philippians 4:6, 7), and surely we can lay down and sleep without being tormented, worried, sleepless, disturbed or uncertain.

Starting the day with the Lord, living it in His way, walking in and embracing His mighty Word that teaches us how to live without fear and in wisdom, and keeping it on our hearts, goes a far way in shaping how we end the day. When we say our prayers and commune with God on our beds, pouring out our hearts to Him we can turn over to Him our sleep, safety and deliverance. We can confidently relinquish our every care to His waking eye, thank Him for the many blessings of the day and we can then sleep sweet as per the Words of Scripture, "When thou liest down, thou shalt not be afraid: yea, thou shalt lie down, and thy sleep shall be sweet" (Proverbs 3:24). God intends for us to enjoy our sleep and not fill it with worry and anxiety. "It is vain for you to rise up early, to sit up late, to eat the bread of sorrows: for He giveth His beloved sleep" (Psalm 127:2), and since He neither slumbers nor sleep (Psalm 121:3, 4) we are to cast all our concerns on Him and His watchful eye will guard and protect us. This same God who brought us through the day, will He not keep us through the night? And when we awake we are with Him and satisfied with His likeness (Psalm 139:18 and Psalm 17:15). "It is of the Lord's mercies that we are not consumed, because His compassions fail not. They are new every morning: great is His faithfulness" (Lamentations 3:22, 23), and if by His divine providence He chooses to return or take us to Himself while we sleep, it would then be our souls awakening to hear and bear witness to the fulfillment of His Word. The child's prayer sought this comfort.

We can sleep sweet and we can sleep in peace and safety because we were awake in God's presence, cared for by His love, sheltered under the shadow of His wings, surrounded by his tender mercies, resting in His everlasting arms and we know that surely the Lord is with us and has put gladness in our hearts.

"For God had not appointed us to wrath, but to obtain salvation by our Lord Jesus Christ, who died for us, that whether we wake or sleep, we should live together with Him" (1 Thessalonians 5:9, 10).

BE BLESSED TODAY AND SLEEP WELL TONIGHT

Pressing On

Every rung on the ladder of life gets higher and higher, every step we take gets firmer and firmer, every resolve grows surer and surer as we press onward for the prize of the high calling in Jesus Christ. And there's no turning back. Thanks Be to God.

LIBERTY AND FREEDOM

"Stand fast therefore in the liberty wherewith Christ hath made us free . . ." (Galatians 5:1)

We observe a great time of celebration, festivity, fireworks, music, gatherings and nationalistic nostalgia in grand commemoration of July 4th. During the last celebration when all the excitement had died down, I could not help but think on and be thankful for the reality of the Words found in Galatians 5:1 which invites the true believers to celebrate what Jesus did at Calvary to secure their freedom. The words are simple, instructive and profound. They call our attention to a three-dimensional celebration which goes on every day of the believer's life. The believer is 1) celebrating their liberation from the law in that Christ paid in full for their sins and they are no longer condemned; 2) they are also celebrating God's free gift of salvation which is their freedom from the bondage of sin and spiritual death and their rebirth into a new spiritual life in Christ.

Can you hear the band playing for such an occasion, "Hallelujah! Hallelujah! Jesus set me free?"

We are called to "stand fast" in that liberty, that means we are to be sure of it, believing in faith on Christ's atoning work on the cross, we are to be firm and unshaken in our faith and in our testimony and we are to hold on to sound doctrine as taught in the Scriptures "For ye shall know the truth and the truth shall make you free" (John 8:32).

The second part of Galatians 5:1 instructs us not to be entangled again with the yoke of bondage. This makes the price for liberty and freedom of the utmost worth as true believers live as a new creation in Christ, disentangled from sin and without turning again to the weak and beggarly elements of it, or having a desire to return to such bondage (Galatians 4:9).

The third dimension of this celebration is that believers are free to love God for His grace and mercy toward them and this is best done by adhering to the Words of Jesus, "If you love Me keep My commandments" (John 14:15). As we live unto God, in obedience to His Word, we express His worthiness and show our love for Him by not using our liberty for an occasion to fall to the flesh and be destructive, but to live in the fullness of God's Spirit in love and service to Him and others (Galatians 5:13).

"If the Son therefore shall make you free, you shall be free indeed" (John 8:36).

BE BLESSED TODAY AND WALK IN THE FREEDOM THAT CHRIST PROVIDED FROM THE BONDAGE OF SIN

*I*N RETROSPECT

"If it had not been the Lord who was on our side . . . Our Help is in the Lord, who made heaven and earth" (Psalm 124:1-8)

As one year comes to a close and another unfolds, what are our thoughts and feelings? In retrospect, what can we leave behind and what can we take forward into the coming year?

Were we uplifted and guided by God's merciful hand?

Were our needs met?

Were we clothed, housed and fed?

Were we employed?

Were our souls satisfied with God's goodness?

Were our souls delighted with God's comforts?

Did we enjoy reasonable health?

Did we forgive others as we were forgiven?

Did we diligently share God's Word?

Did we walk in the ways of the Lord?

Have we grown spiritually?

Can we say with all assuredness that God is our refuge and strength, a very present help in trouble? Is He our portion for ever, our strength and saving grace, our rock and defense, high tower, shield and buckler, our peace and truly our expectation is from Him? Can we say I will love thee O Lord, My strength? Can we clap our hands and shout unto

God with the voice of triumph, that He alone is worthy of all the praise. He is the same yesterday, today and forever and will be the same God in the New Year as He was in the old.

In retrospect, can we say yes! And thank You, God. It is only because of your love and watchful eye, safety and tender care, that we made it this far and through this year, even when it seemed that our steps had almost slipped, You were there, leading, guiding, encouraging, comforting, providing, blessing, faithful.

Are we committed to leaving those things behind that are not conducive to healthy Christian growth, and an abiding faithful walk with God? Let us then put aside all malice, anger, wrath, hypocrisies, envy and evil speaking (Colossians 3:5-8) and put on, therefore, as the elect of God, holy and beloved, bowels of mercies, kindness, humbleness, meekness, longsuffering and let the peace of God rule in our hearts and the Word of Christ dwell in us richly (Colossians 3:15, 16) as we move forward to grow in grace and stature and in the knowledge of God to live Godly lives. In looking back on what was, can we now look forward and press toward the mark for the prize of the high calling of God in Christ Jesus? (Philippians 3:14).

In retrospect, we can ask and confirm that if it had not been for great Almighty God on our side, where would we be? Unless the Lord had been our help, our soul had almost dwelt in silence (Psalm 94:17).

"Thou hast dealt well with Thy servant, O Lord, according to Thy Word" (Psalm 119:65).

BE BLESSED TODAY AND HOLD TO GOD'S UNCHANGING HAND

*D*RESSED FOR BATTLE

"Put on the whole armor of God, that ye may be able to stand against the wiles of the devil" (Ephesians 6:11)

The verses of Scripture found in Ephesians 6:10-18 are remarkable in their teaching. They emphasize the reality that the devil is alive and well and his modus operandi is carved in calculated, crafty and cunning methods also known as wiles or schemes. 1 Peter 5:8 reminds us that the devil walks around as a roaring lion seeking whom he may devour and God warns us to be sober and vigilant against him and to put on God's whole armor that we may be able to stand firmly against the wiles of such a foe.

In recognition of this, and lest we be misguided in our approach or understanding of this fact, God points out that we wrestle not against flesh and blood which may appear to be doing the work of the devil, but against principalities, against powers, against the rulers of the darkness of this world, against spiritual wickedness in high places (Ephesians 6:12). These all sum up to be the work of the devil who does not necessarily show up as a bad day, illness or misfortune, but as a strong, powerful and evil entity, a ruler of darkness (Colossians 1:13; 1 Thessalonians 5:5), an accuser of the brethren (Revelations 12:10), a subtle tempter (Genesis 3; Matthew 4) and definitely as spiritual wickedness in high places. The high places in our lives are those things that we establish and exalt above God which rule and capture the best seat of our heart and give the devil a foothold to sow and harvest his schemes.

Therefore, God has given the true believers the ability to live each day completely equipped and outfitted with spiritual weaponry to ward off the devil, to overcome him, to be spiritual morticians and put to death the deeds of the flesh which are devil-oriented and instead, be led by the spirit of God (Romans 8:12-14). We are spiritually dressed to stand firmly against the methods of the devil and to withstand his maneuvers, and we do so by taking unto ourselves the whole armor of God, and having done all that, we stand strong in the Lord (Ephesians 6:13).

To be dressed in God's armor, as set out in Ephesians 6:11-17, is not to accumulate an inventory of weaponry waiting to be picked up and put on and to be used when needed to fight our battles. God gives this armor to His elect at the time of their salvation and like the baptism of the Holy Spirit and all the spiritual gifts that they receive, the armor of God is weaved into their innermost parts and is an indwelling disposition crucial to the Christian's survival in a sin-filled and satan-dominated world. It is the characteristic of the saved and it helps them to be victorious and more than conquerors as they fight the good fight of faith through the power of Jesus Christ. We are to remember that the battle is the Lords, for it is He who fights for us, it is He who executes judgment on the devil, it is He who wages the war against satan and his schemes to keep us bound in sin and out of God's hands. We cannot put satan away, only God can. Romans 16:20 tells us that "the God of peace shall bruise satan under your feet shortly." He is on a tentative leash and God will take care of him on our behalf. We are to be just God's children, fortified in our positions, dressed for the battle and then we stand still and see the salvation of the Lord.

We stand dressed with our loins girded about with truth, and wearing the breastplate of righteousness. Truth and sincerity are the Christian's disposition and as Christ is girded in righteousness, so are to be His children. Our feet are to be shod with the preparation of the Gospel of peace. We are to take the shield of faith, wherewith we shall be able to quench or put out all the fiery darts of the wicked and we are to take the helmet of salvation, and the sword of the Spirit, which is the Word of God (Ephesians 6:14-17). This inventory of spiritual armor is Christ Himself. We are adorned with Him, who is the way, the truth and the life (John 14:6).

We are standing firm on God's Word and ready to adhere to it as the rule and centerfold of our lives, with our feet well placed and balanced against the challenges that may prevail and we are ready to take the Gospel of peace as ambassadors of Christ out into the world (Matthew 28:19, 20; Ephesians 6:19, 20). "How beautiful are the feet of them that preach the Gospel of peace, and bring glad tidings of good things" (Romans 10:15 and Isaiah 52:7). Christ is our faith and we take Him everywhere, trusting in His mercies, His Word and promises that fortify and strengthen us to extinguish all negativity of the wicked one. Our faith is a defensive piece of armor we use to fight those unguarded moments that we may have that can allow the devil to slip in and take hold. Without this faith (Christ), it is impossible to please God (Hebrews 11:6).

The helmet of salvation is placed on our heads and we are covered by the sacrificial blood of Jesus so that nothing can ever separate us from His love (Romans 8:35-39), and we wear it to show that we bear His mark. "Therefore, if any man be in Christ he is a new creature" (2 Corinthians 5:17). We carry the sword of the Spirit which is the Word of God, quick and powerful and sharper than any two-edged sword (Hebrews 4:12), and it is our offensive armor and weapon to fight back. Jesus used it against the devil when He was tempted in the wilderness (Matthew 4:4-11). We are to continually feast on God's Word as the sole authority of our lives and hide it in our hearts so that we might not sin against Him (Psalm 119:11; Proverbs 4:21). We are to study to show ourselves approved unto God (2 Timothy 2:15). We are to be on guard sanctifying God in our hearts and be always ready to give an answer to every man that asks a reason of the hope that we have (1 Peter 3:15). And we are to be buffeted in prayer - praying always with all prayer and supplication in the Spirit for ourselves and for others (Ephesians 6:18).

As new creatures in Christ, we have the imperative to take the whole armor of God, not just parts of it. It comes as a complete package, like the fruit of the Spirit listed in Galatians

5:22, one is minimized and can be ineffective without the other. If we take one and neglect the other, we run the risk of being exposed and defeated and having a shaky testimony. As children of God we are complete in all His offerings and we do not have to rush into battle but be on guard and prepared for it. We can stand in faith, knowing that God is in control. We are dressed in His character to slay whatever seeks to confuse and destroy the truth of the Gospel and the life we desire to live as pleasing unto God. We will also remain dressed in this armor until the time of Christ's return and at that time we will still be able to stand firmly with God and see His glory and judgment revealed. "A thousand shall fall at thy side, and ten thousand at thy right hand, but it shall not come near thee. Only with thine eyes shalt thou behold and see the reward of the wicked. Because thou hast made the Lord, even the most high thy habitation" (Psalm 91: 7-9).

"The night is far spent, the day is at hand: let us therefore cast off the works of darkness, and let us put on the armor of light" (Romans 13:12).

BE BLESSED TODAY AND FULLY DRESSED IN GOD'S PROTECTIVE GEAR

*I*TCHING EARS

"For the time will come, when they will not endure sound doctrine; but after their own lusts shall they heap to themselves teachers, having itching ears" (2 Timothy 4:3)

The Bible is absolutely trustworthy. It is God's Word and standard for our lives and is extremely accurate in describing our frailties and dispositions. If we ever want to have a true glimpse of ourselves, we should consult the Bible. However, despite its validity and inerrancy and its discerning of the thoughts and intents of the heart, there are some who do not believe or accept everything it teaches as God-breathed, and there are others who entirely discount its wonderful message and are happy replacing its Words of truth with inaccuracies and false doctrines that are easy to hear and bear.

During His earthly mission, as Jesus went about teaching, He encountered those who were astonished, appalled, upset and doubtful at His message of truth and seized every opportunity to contradict, oppose, trick, revile and even hurt Him. He spoke as one with authority, and yet much of what He said was vehemently opposed and challenged by the teachers of the law, because it exposed their hypocrisies, pricked their consciences and was not the leaven of compromise, ease or restriction that they were willing to hear.

And so it is today. God warned of this phenomenon, that people of this day will demonstrate their desire to hear

151

and absorb anything but the true Gospel. They will find it expedient, convenient and comfortable to hear a subliminal message that promotes gaiety, peace and well-being, ease and success, riches and fame, blessings, prosperity and accomplishments, security and safety. They prefer the "do it yourself and save yourself without God" gospel and a little bit of God and much of the world as their yardstick, as well as many other contrived platitudes scripted to bear man's words and not God's. These are all exuberantly proclaimed from many quarters to itching ears. That means to ears that shut down at the sound of truth and perk up and twitch gleefully at language that titillates the sensual rather than the spiritual and penetrate similarly itching and adamant hearts. "But they refused to hearken (hear and believe) and pulled away the shoulder, and stopped (closed) their ears, that they should not hear" (Zechariah 7:11).

As we focus on the infallibility of the Scripture, we must look at God's Words through His prophet Jeremiah which state "The prophets prophesy falsely, and the priests bear rule by their means; and my people love to have it so: and what will ye do in the end thereof?" (Jeremiah 5:31). God elaborates on the condition of the sinful heart "that when they (unbelievers) knew God, they did not glorify Him, neither were thankful; but became vain and darkened in their hearts, professing themselves to be wise, they became fools who changed the truth of God into a lie and worshipped and served the creature more than the Creator and who knowing the judgment of God, that they which commit such things are worthy of death, not only do the same, but have pleasure in them that do them" (Romans 1:21-32). In other words, those following after their own lusts who turn away their ears from truth and unto fables, and who have itching ears to hear what they want, shall heap to themselves deceitfulness or attract those spurting the wrong type of gospel and will condone and encourage rebellion against the Word of God. ". . . They have ears to hear and hear not, for they are a rebellious house" (Ezekiel 12:2).

Jesus taught extensively in parables. Scripture tells us that with many such parables He spoke the Word unto them, as they were able to hear it. But without a parable He did not speak (Matthew 13:34; Mark 4:33, 34). But He also opened ears to hear and eyes to see and hearts to receive. And after many of his teachings, he concluded with the Words "He that hath ears to hear let him hear" (Matthew 11:15, 13:9, 43; Mark 4:9, 23, 7:16; Luke 14:35). This is because the natural man receives not the things of the Spirit of God; for they are foolishness unto him; neither can he know them, because they are spiritually discerned (1 Corinthians 2:14). When Jesus was alone with His disciples, He would expound all His sayings to them. "For unto them (and the true believers), it is given to know the mystery of the kingdom of God: but unto them that are without (the unsaved), all these things are done in parables that seeing they may see, and not perceive; and hearing they may hear, and not understand . . ." (Mark 4:11, 12).

153

As children of God, we are always to be seeking after truth. When the Word of God pierces our ears and arrests our heart, we are to be willing to let it sink to the point of our deepest need. "So then faith comes by hearing and hearing by the Word of God" (Romans 10:17). We are not to shrink away from its truth and replace it with doctrines that bear a false witness and blind our hearts from an obedient, committed and fulfilling walk with God. David the sweet Psalmist sought after truth, no matter how harsh, convicting or chastising it was. He repeatedly prayed to be led in God's truth and to be taught the way of His statutes (Psalm 25:5, 40:11, 43:3, 86:11 and 119:33-40). He prayed for truth in his innermost parts and understanding of God's Word so that his life would please God. His ears itched for the true Gospel and so should ours.

As we serve God, let us try the spirits whether they are of God (1 John 4:1), let us lay hold of sound doctrine, learn truth, walk in the richness of God's Word and open our hearts to greatly desire and meditate on it. If there be any doubt of the Scripture lurking in our hearts and if our ears are inclined in a different direction, O let us, therefore, pray for God's guidance and His touch on those wayward spots. For God promises that if we would not hear Him, He would not hear when we cry (Zechariah 7:13), and those who bring damnable heresies and cater to itching ears will bring upon themselves swift destruction (2 Peter 2:1).

"Apply thine heart unto instruction, and thine ears to the Words of knowledge" (Proverbs 23:12).

BE BLESSED TODAY WITH ITCHING EARS TO HEAR AND EAGER HEARTS TO RECEIVE SOUND DOCTRINE

Seventy Times Seven

"For if ye forgive men their trespasses, your heavenly Father will also forgive you" (Matthew 6:14)

The Bible is replete with teachings on forgiveness. The word forgive is used as many as fifty-six times in the Old and New Testaments. Its most poignant use is found in the Lord's Prayer. The disciples asked Jesus to teach them to pray, and He did indeed. (Luke 11:1-4). In this prayer, Jesus teaches that when we pray we are to ask for God's forgiveness of our sins as we ourselves stand ready to forgive others who trespass (offend) against us. Jesus relates parables that teach the importance of genuine forgiveness of others as a result of our own forgiveness (Matthew 18:23-25) and also as a prerequisite to seeking our own (Matthew 5:23, 24).

This must have been resting heavily on the Apostle Peter's heart. For on one occasion, Peter came to Jesus and said "Lord, how often shall my brother sin against me, and I forgive him? till seven times?" And Jesus answered him saying "I say not unto thee, until seven times: but, until seventy times seven" (Matthew 18:21, 22). This response has puzzled many. Why seventy times seven? Does it mean that we are to count each offense against us and forgive each person that offends us up to 490 times and then stop at the 491st time? Certainly not. We would have a lot of scoring to do. God frequently uses numbers in the Bible to illustrate spiritual truths. Seven is one such number that God uses to teach of the perfect fulfillment of His purpose, and Jesus uses this number in an accelerated way to exemplify God's purpose for us to be of the same heart as He is in showing mercy toward others without keeping score, as we desire the same for ourselves. God is forgiving and has forgiven the sins of those whom He has saved, and not only has He forgiven sins, but He remembers them no more. "For as far as the east is from the west, so far has He removed our transgressions from us" (Psalm 103:12). "I am He (God) that blotteth out thy transgressions for My own sake, and will not remember thy sins" (Isaiah 43:25; Jeremiah 31:34). "For I will be merciful to their unrighteousness, and their sins and iniquities will I remember no more" (Hebrews 8:12 and 10:17). "Who is a God like unto Thee that pardons iniquity … and delights in mercy" (Micah 7:18).

So the power in our ability to forgive is to be ad infinitum. We are to keep on forbearing and forgiving one another no matter how difficult it seems. Each time that we forgive or are tempted not to forgive someone, we are to remember that we have been forgiven by God and by others. This is the teaching in the Lord's Prayer. And if we are inclined to be resentful, unforgiving, intolerant and proud, we must consider the advice of Scripture to examine ourselves, whether we be in the faith and prove ourselves. (2 Corinthians 13:5). For as God by His tender mercies has forgiven us, so are we with deep gratitude, as new creations in Christ, redeemed, sanctified and obedient are to forgive others.

Seventy times seven reminds us that if we confess our sins, God is faithful and just to forgive us our sins and to cleanse us from all our unrighteousness (1 John 1:9). Seventy times seven teaches us that today, we are to extend the olive branch of peace and forgiveness to all who may offend us and free ourselves from an unforgiving spirit, guilt, anger and pain so that we can be at peace with others and with God and can come boldly to the throne room of His grace, where we can find His help for our need. It tells us that if we bring our gift to the altar and there remember that our brother has something against us, that we are to take the first step and leave our gift and go and make amends, reconcile and forgive and then return to offer our gift to God (Matthew 5:23, 24). Seventy times seven means we are to always be ready to offer to another that special quality which the child of God possesses. We are to stop counting and start forgiving and move on because our hearts are large enough to offer it. We are not to withhold good from them to whom it is due, when it is in the power of our hand to do it (Proverbs 3:27).

Is there some one to whom we should be reaching out? Let us then make the move, make the call, make the prayer. We do so not because we have been good or perfect and without fault, but because we have tasted of God's mercy toward us. We have been forgiven.

"And when ye stand praying, forgive, if ye have anything against anyone: that your Father also which is in heaven may forgive you your trespasses. But if ye do not forgive, neither will your Father which is in heaven forgive your trespasses" (Mark 11:25, 26).

BE BLESSED TODAY AS YOUR HEART IS FREE FROM THE BURDEN OF UNFORGIVENESS

*T*HE RACE

"Know ye not that they which run in a race run all, but one receiveth the prize? So run, that ye may obtain"
(1 Corinthians 9:24)

This past week, like many of you, I went to the Olympics, and witnessed from the comfort of my home, the drama, the cheers and groans, the challenges of sportsmanship, the disappointments at losing, the exhilaration of winning and the performance of some amazing feats. It was all about gold, silver, bronze or nothing at all. Each time I found myself getting excited at the outcome of an event, the verse of Scripture from 1 Corinthians 9:24, quoted above, kept coming to mind, until I could no longer ignore it and had to focus on its intent.

So what race are we really running? The word race in this text refers not to a competition but to a milestone or a unit of measure, e.g. furlong, as described in the original Greek text. If we are not careful, we can be running the wrong race of life, depending on what the pay off is. As Christians, we are to check our race against the divine instructions given in God's Word. How have we matured in our Christian walk, what milestones have we passed? Have we gained victory over sin in our lives, are we at the same mark as we were yesterday or a year ago? Is our zeal for the things of God?

The Apostle Paul, under the inspiration of the Holy Spirit, takes us down the road of life, where the spiritual race is to be run and it is important that we know how we are doing. Are we in for the one hundred, two hundred or four hundred meters, the sprint, the dash or the relay, the short-run or the long haul? There will be hindrances, roadblocks, set backs and blunders. Who is on our side or breathing hard on our back, what winds of anxiety whip around our ankles? Satan may be creeping up close from the outer lane or from out of left field, as he is still walking around like a roaring lion, seeking to devour and destroy those who have not made God and His Word the authority of their lives. Our race must, therefore, be one of faithfulness and endurance, and we have God's promise of the crown of life (James 1:12; Revelations 2:10).

We are to be dressed in God's armor with our feet shod with the preparation of the true Gospel of peace (Ephesians 6:15) and run with perseverance. God promises that those who endure will receive the incorruptible crown of life (i.e. God Himself) which will not fade away (1 Corinthians 9:25), be recalled or adjudicated. The earthly gains and the gold and silver of this world will all fade away, but God's Word will not (Matthew 24:35). The Psalmist confirmed that God's Word is better than thousands of gold and silver (Psalm 119:72), and it is to be desired more than gold, yea, than much fine gold (Psalm 19:10).

All those who are in Christ and do His Will and resting contented in His grace and provision can make it to the tape and be sure winners. So, therefore, let us run this race with perseverance looking unto Jesus, the author and finisher of our faith (Hebrews 12:2). Forgetting those things which are behind, and reaching forth unto those things which are before, let us press forward toward the mark for the prize of the high calling of God in Christ Jesus, keeping our eyes on the prize of eternal life (Philippians 3:13, 14) – that crown of righteousness that would not fade away.

As we run this earthly race to the eternal finish line, confidently, courageously and Godly, we are strengthened to do all things through Christ (Philippians 4:13) and we do all to the glory of God (1 Corinthians 10:31). Let us not drop the baton of faith, beat the air, or run uncertainly. Let us not fail to pass on God's Word truthfully and responsibly to those whose hands are outstretched, and for those who would receive it, be sure to hold firm to its truths which cannot be shaken. Thanks be to God, which giveth us the victory through our Lord Jesus Christ (1 Corinthians 15:57). We can then affirm like Paul:

"I have fought a good fight, I have finished my course, I have kept the faith: Henceforth there is laid up for me a crown of righteousness, which the Lord, the righteous judge, shall give me at that day: and not to me only, but unto all them also that love His appearing" (2 Timothy 4:7, 8).

RUN AND BE BLESSED TODAY

BURNING QUESTIONS

Can we by searching find the ways of God?
Can we by asking get truth?
Can we by seeking find life?
Some say there are more questions than answers
but God says for every question you have – I am
the answer.

WHAT IS STANDING BETWEEN YOU AND GOD?

". . . Come take up the cross, and follow Me" (Mark 10:21)

The Gospels of Matthew, Mark and Luke all record the story of the rich young ruler (see Mark 10:17-31, Matthew19:16-30 and Luke 18:18-27). It was important enough for the Lord to have it recounted by three of His disciples. We see the rich young ruler having everything but lacking a very necessary ingredient – a close walk with Jesus. Jesus told us that to be His friend we have to give up the world (1 John 2:15-17). He told the rich young ruler to sell all he had and come follow Him. This made the young ruler sorrowful. It was too much for him to do. Scripture tells us he turned away. He missed the opportunity of a life-changing blessing by not following Christ. Jesus remarked in Mark 10:25, that "it is easier for a camel to go through the eye of a needle than for a rich man to enter the kingdom of God." The eye of a needle was a gate in the wall in Jerusalem. It was a very small opening and merchants had to unsaddle their camels to pass through this gate. The comparison Jesus makes tells us that with all our riches, we cannot enter the kingdom of God. We have to unsaddle our trappings and our possessions. Verse 23 says "how hardly shall they that have riches enter into the kingdom of God", that means "with what great difficulty." We can compare this with God's warning in Matthew 7:13 "Enter ye in at the strait gate: for wide is the gate, and broad is the way, that leads to destruction, and many there be which go in thereat: Because strait is the gate, and narrow is the way, which leads unto life, and few there be that find it." Indeed, it is with great difficulty that many persons will not make it to heaven because they allow material things to stand between them and Christ. 1 Timothy 6:10-12 and 17-19 gives us a stern warning on loving money and putting our trust in material things and uncertain riches, and encourages us to lay up for ourselves a good foundation for eternal life. Mark 10:21 gives us an indication that all was not lost for this rich young ruler. It tells us that Jesus loved him. Perhaps he was given another chance and not utterly cast out. Psalm 37:23 and 24 tells us that the steps of a good man are ordered by the Lord and though he fall (which seems to be the case of the young ruler) he will not be utterly cast out. For the Lord upholds him with His hand.

We thank God for this good news for each of us who may be clutching to something other than God, that we can release its grip and hold fast to Christ. And so I beg the question – What is standing between us and God? Is it money, pride, wisdom, family, friends, habits, anxieties, fear, sin, our will, or just plain us? Whatever it is, we should not wait until it is too late to find out where we stand, but use this text as good and sound guidance for us to give up the world and follow Jesus. And as we turn our eyes and fix them on Him, the things of the world will grow strangely dim, as the hymn writer[4] penned.

"For what shall it profit a man, if he shall gain the whole world, and lose his own soul" (Mark 8:36).

BE BLESSED TODAY AND SET NOTHING BETWEEN YOU AND THE SAVIOR

WHAT DOES THE LORD REQUIRE OF THEE?

"He hath shewed thee, O man, what is good; and what doth the Lord require of thee, but to do justly, and to love mercy, and to walk humbly with thy God?" (Micah 6:8)

Far too often, we attach ourselves to things, events and works and label them as what God wants from us. We may expend much time and energy following our own devices and plans convinced that we are offering to God things that matter and are important to Him, when in actuality they are not.

We must be careful to not make our boast in our own prescriptions done in the name of the Lord. Scripture is clear that we are not saved by our works of righteousness, but only by God's gift of grace through faith (Ephesians 2:8, 9). However, once we have become saved, we are saved unto good works as Christ's workmanship that God has ordained for us to walk in (Ephesians 2:10). Those good works that we then do are devoid of our own label and are to be a light shining before men and glorifying God in heaven (Matthew 5:16). What should these good works include or entail?

David had found out the hard way that any sacrificial or personal offerings which did not align to God's desires were useless. Under the inspiration of the Holy Spirit he penned the most contrite Psalm 51 and shares with us in verse 16, that the Lord does not require the outward offering of sacrifice or burnt offerings that he might feel inclined to give as an appeasement to Him. He understood that it was only through a broken and a contrite heart that he could have an entrance to God and present himself desolate and repentant. "The sacrifices of God are a broken spirit: a broken and a contrite heart, O God, Thou wilt not despise" (Psalm 51:17).

In the Book of Micah from which our Scripture text comes, the teaching is quite clear as to what God requires from us. Micah wants to be sure that his offerings and those of others are in keeping with what God wants and asks the following: "Wherewith shall I come before the Lord, and bow myself before the high God? Shall I come before him with burnt offerings, with calves of a year old? Will the Lord be pleased with thousands of rams, or with ten thousands of rivers of oil? Shall I give my firstborn for my transgression, the fruit of my body for the sin of my soul?" (Micah 6:6-7). Micah clearly recognizes that the tangible physical offerings of man's hands are not what God is interested in or what He requires.

In the Old Testament, sacrificial offerings were the way of life, given to God as a way for atoning for one's sin. However, when Jesus Christ went to the cross and shed His blood for the sins of many, sacrificial offerings became null and void. No longer can one come before God with the blood of rams or cows or even the offerings of their first born (as God had requested of Abraham in Genesis 22), or with their own perceived works of righteousness. Clearly, God is interested in the pure and undefiled offerings of our hearts and this is the spiritual intent of these examples.

The Bible gives accounts of many persons who did good works in the name of the Lord. Such work was not done for their own benefit and to put them in the spotlight but from hearts that were conformed to God's will (Acts 9:36). Others who sought to do works as a means of show or extracting gain were punished (Acts Chapters 5 and 8; 1 Kings 18). However, the true believer will find that their best work is borne out of knowing God's will by studying His Holy Scriptures which are given for their instruction in righteousness and for them to be completely outfitted unto all good works (2 Timothy 3:16, 17).

In handing down the commandments to the people of Israel, Moses makes a similar statement to what God requires of His people. We read the following in Deuteronomy 10:12, 13, "And now, Israel, what doth the Lord thy God require of thee, but to fear the Lord thy God, to walk in all His ways, and to love Him, and to serve the Lord thy God with all thy heart and with all thy soul and to keep the commandments of the Lord, and His statutes. . ."

We may not be offering rams and bullocks, but our works and offerings that exclude God's requirements do not honor Him. We must be careful not to be caught up in the frenzy of doing works as a way of capturing God's attention and engineering His blessings, while we fail to obey His commandments. He does not look at the outward appearance but on the inward condition of the heart and because of this what we offer to God must be in strict adherence to what He requires of us. ". . . and what doth the Lord require of thee, but to do justly, and to love mercy, and to walk humbly with thy God" (Micah 6:8).

There is no hint of a tangible offering in this three-fold prescription, but a call to examine our hearts and our intentions whether they align with that of God's. We are to do justly because we serve a just God (Deuteronomy 32:4 and Isaiah 45:21), we are to love mercy because God's mercies follow us all the days of our lives (Psalm 23:6), they endure forever (Psalm 136), and are new every morning (Lamentations 3:22, 23). We are to walk humbly with God and be clothed in humility, being absolutely dependent upon Him because God resists the proud and gives grace to the humble (1 Peter 5:5; James 4:10; Isaiah 57:15). God desires and requires that we walk according to His commandments and we show our love for Him by keeping them (John 14:15). "For this is the love of God, that we keep His commandments: and His commandments are not grievous (burdensome)" (1 John 5:3). Our whole duty then is to fear God, (that is to approach Him with a wholesome respect and awe) and keep his commandments (Ecclesiastes 12:13).

"And whatsoever you do, do it heartily as to the Lord, and not unto men; knowing that of the Lord ye shall receive the reward of the inheritance: for ye serve the Lord Christ" (Colossians 3:23, 24).

BE BLESSED TODAY. WHAT THE LORD REQUIRES OF US, THIS IS WHAT WE BRING TO HIM

WHO CAN UNDERSTAND HIS ERRORS?

"Who can understand his errors? Cleanse thou me from secret faults" (Psalm 19:12)

The Psalmist asks a most relevant and important question. "Who can understand his errors?" It shows his desire to confront and know his weaknesses, his frailties, his short comings, and those dispositions that would cause him to stumble, trip and sin.

This searching question comes in the middle of his remarkable testimony about the power of God's Word which is able to convert the soul and make wise the simple (Psalm 19:7), rejoice the heart and enlighten the eyes (Psalm 19:8). He continues that the fear of the Lord is clean, enduring for ever: the judgments of the Lord are true and righteous altogether (Psalm 19:9) and God's Words are to be desired than much fine gold and in keeping of them there is great reward (Psalm 19:10, 11). He recognizes that God's Word is able to do more for him and for us, than any other word can. All Scripture is given by inspiration of God and is profitable for doctrine, for reproof, for correction and for instruction in righteousness (2 Timothy 3:16), and in the light of what the Psalmist knows about God and His Word, he begs the question for himself and certainly for us "Who can understand his errors?"

We can restate the question like this, "Why is light given to a man whose way is hid, and whom God hath hedged in?" and "O God, Thou knowest my foolishness; and my sins are not hid from Thee." We know that there is nothing about us that is hidden from God and therefore, we should not disguise, compromise, cover up or perpetuate our errors. For he that follows after righteousness and mercy finds life, righteousness, and honor (Proverbs 21:21), he that covers his sins shall not prosper: but whoso confesses and forsakes them shall have mercy (Proverbs 28:13), and while our ways may seem right in our own eyes, the Lord indeed ponders and takes note of our heart (Proverbs 21:2). He sees our ways, and counts all our steps (Job 31:4).

The ways in which we can understand our errors are by first and foremost believing the Scripture's testimony "For all have sinned and come short of the glory of God" (Romans 3:23), and acknowledging them for what they are "For I acknowledge my transgressions: and my sin is ever before me" (Psalm 51:3) and to whom they are committed. "Against Thee only (God) have I sinned and done this evil in thy sight . . ." (Psalm 51:4).

God's Word will abide in strong hearts and help overcome the wicked one (1 John 2:14). So let us ask God to cleanse us from any secret faults and create in us a clean heart and renew in us a right spirit (Psalm 51:10) as we intentionally seek to cleanse our way by taking heed according to His Word and not wander from its teachings, hiding it in our hearts so that we might not sin against God (Psalm 119:9-11).

The Word of God will reveal and help us to understand and correct our errors as we study to show ourselves approved unto God (2 Timothy 2:15); as we examine ourselves whether we be in the faith (2 Corinthians 13:5) and hold fast to sound doctrine, and above all as we incline our ears to God's sayings, keeping them before our eyes and in the midst of our heart (Proverbs 4:21). Our prayer should pattern the Psalmist "Lord make me to know my end and the measure of my days that I may know how frail I am" (Psalm 39:4).

". . . Ye do err, not knowing the Scriptures, nor the power of God" (Matthew 22:29).

BE BLESSED TODAY AS YOU MEDITATE ON GOD'S WORD AND HIDE IT IN YOUR HEART

WHAT! NEVER THIRST AGAIN?

No! Never thirst again. What! Never thirst again? No! Never thirst again.

"Therefore with joy shall ye draw water out of the wells of salvation" (Isaiah 14:23)

There is a well in Sychar that bears testimony to an event that opened up the way and teaching of the supernatural quenching of the human spiritual thirst.

Jesus was passing through Samaria and in the city of Sychar He met a woman coming to draw water from Jacob's well where He had stopped to rest. It was a hot day and He was thirsty and asked her for a drink. She was surprised at His request and asked Him how was it that He a Jew would ask her a Samaritan woman for anything, much less a drink, because the Jews had no dealings with the Samaritans (see John 4:5-9).

Then in a remarkable turn of events the offer of the gift of God was given to her. Jesus told her if she knew who it was that was requesting the drink she would turn the question around and ask for a drink from Him. He promised her what she was never promised before. He offered her what she never had before and what she never knew she needed. Like many of us today, she seemed contented with her own thirst of the world and ways of relieving its self-perpetuating grip. He offered her living water, and not just a sip but a deluge that would spring up within her into everlasting life (John 4:14).

He offered her the pure water of the Gospel. He offered her Himself, the life-giving flow.

And she wisely and excitedly asked for it. "Sir, give me this water that I thirst not?" Are we asking for the water of life? Are we seeking to have our spiritual thirst quenched? And not with food or water or that which creates more thirst, but with that which runs from the pure source and lavishly wells up within us into a newness of life eternal. Such a filling produces a lasting contentment in Jesus Christ, the giver of every good and perfect gift and the joy of man's desires.

Come to the well and see a man! His name is Jesus. He will water you with His Word that will forever be a lamp unto your feet and a light unto your path and make you lay aside your own acquired thirst quenchers. Come to the well and meet the fountain's head who will give you water that you would not have to draw. Come to the well and meet the One who is able to rebirth you with His water and His Spirit, so that you can enter into the kingdom of heaven. Come to the well and come empty handed, so your hands will be filled with goodness. Come broken, so that you can be mended and restored to a wholeness you never knew. Come eager to receive in faith, the greatest filling of righteousness you will ever have so that you will never hunger or thirst again. "He that believeth on me, as the Scripture hath said, out of his belly shall flow rivers of living water" (John 7:38).

Come! See a man, which will tell you all things that you ever did, and forgive your sins and give you His peace. Is

175

not this the Christ? Yes, it is. And the living water He offers will transform you into the true worshipper that God is seeking. One whose heart is bowed in spirit and truth (John 4:22-24).

". . . And let him that is athirst come. And whosoever will, let him take the water of life freely" (Revelation 22:17).

BE BLESSED TODAY AND DRINK FROM THE WELLSPRING OF LIFE

WHY SPEND MONEY?

**"HO, every one that thirsts, come ye to the waters, and he
that hath no money; come ye, buy, and eat; yea, come buy
wine and milk without money and without price.
Wherefore do ye spend money for that which is not bread?
. . ." (Isaiah 55:1, 2)**

God asks this question from His sovereign vantage
point of wisdom, maturity and knowledge of what is useful,
needed, and important and has great worth for us. The things
that attract us are usually fleeting and of great price and with
each new enticement, invention and innovation, we are known
to spend money excessively on such perishables.

God invites our attention to, and interest in His
storehouse of eternal treasures which are free for the asking.
There is no dollar value to the recipients; the price has already
been paid by Jesus Christ. The catalog is open, the statements
are valid, there is no fine print or hidden message and the
invitation is given to come buy, come eat, come buy wine and
milk without money and without price. And we should be
flocking to such a bargain because the wine and milk referred
to are not the literal perishable commodities of the land but the
eternal, saving Gospel of grace of our Lord Jesus Christ.

The question is asked "Why spend money for that
which is not bread?" In other words, why are our priorities
misplaced? Why is our focus misdirected? Why are we
craving for and expending our all on those things that do not

177

give life and on that which will not suffice? Jesus is the bread of life and we are to seek after Him. His food is free, righteous and peaceable and we are to lay hold on it for ourselves. And even those without money can buy, for He promises the kingdom of Heaven to the blessed poor in spirit (Matthew 5:3). This and all God's promises are true because His Word shall not return void to Him, but shall accomplish that which He pleases, and it shall prosper in the thing whereto He sent it (Isaiah 55:11).

Each season ignites its own commercial cheer and by worldly standards people are hyped up to acquire the latest gadgets and fashions and to spend money on assorted items and pleasures to give themselves a good feeling. God cautions us to not spend money for that which is not bread and which does not satisfy the deepest longing of our souls. If we know Jesus and walk in daily fellowship with Him, we will have the feeling, the ecstasy and contentment of His grace, and the water He gives to those who thirst shall be in them a well of water springing up into everlasting life (John 4:14). His invitation is as priceless and meaningful today as it was when first offered. It is the greatest investment we can make without laying down a dime. We should heed the call, especially now, to hearken diligently to God and to eat that which is good and let our souls delight itself in fatness (Isaiah 55:2).

Let us, therefore, taste and see that the Lord is good. Let us celebrate with joy and peace in the Lord Jesus Christ, Savior of mankind, Lion of Judah and soon returning King of glory. Durable riches and honor are with Him. His fruit is better than gold, yea, than fine gold: and His revenue than choice silver. He leads us in the way of righteousness, in the midst of the paths of judgment that He may cause those that love Him to inherit substance and He fills their treasures from His treasures of wisdom and knowledge (Proverbs 8:18-21; Colossians 2:3).

"Come, eat of my bread, and drink of the wine which I have mingled" (Proverbs 9:5).

BE BLESSED TODAY IN THE RICHNESS OF GOD'S FREE GRACE

GIANTS OR GRASSHOPPERS?

"And there we saw the giants, the sons of Anak, which come of the giants: and we were in our own sight as grasshoppers, and so we were in their sight" (Numbers 13:33)

This is a very interesting verse. It is describing how some of the spies that Moses by the commandment of the Lord sent to spy out the land of Canaan, viewed the inhabitants they found there and how they saw themselves in comparison to them. These men returned an evil report of the land which they had searched out and relegated themselves in their own eyes, as well as the eyes of the inhabitants to grasshoppers, while acknowledging those they saw as giants. Is this good or bad?

In the world of positive thinking and motivation such intimidating deference to others may be seen as negative. In the spiritual context, those who went up to check out the land appeared to have relied on their own assessment of the situation rather than trusting God's. Except for Joshua and Caleb, who were strong men of God and who returned an exceeding good report of the land (Numbers 14:6-9), the others were negative and did not see the good God intended for them to see, and this displeased God (Numbers 14:10-16).

We can transpose this experience to some of our own. How do we see the land that God is giving us? This can be in our daily needs and His provision, in our challenges and in His promises of blessedness and eternal salvation. Does it seem inadequate, impenetrable, unreal or far fetched? Do we deflate ourselves to being grasshoppers against the giants of life that we encounter? Or do we take strength in the assurances that we are a chosen generation, a royal priesthood, an holy nation, a peculiar people of God (1 Peter 2:9) who are able to do all things through Christ who gives us the strength (Philippians 4:13), and walk by faith and not by sight? (2 Corinthians 5:7). Do we suffer from the grasshopper mentality, whereby we feel inadequate; we procrastinate and are intimidated by challenges? Are we fearful of change and the unknown and are unable to pick up our cross and follow Christ? Is our faith strong in the Lord and powerful to prayerfully move mountains (Matthew 17:20 and 21:21)? Do we completely trust that with God all things are possible even when we do not have the full picture?

God reminds us that He has not given us the spirit of fear, but of power and of love and of a sound mind (2 Timothy 1:7), therefore, we are to be careful not to belittle ourselves in His own eyes and relegate our abilities to feebleness, and deny the strength of what He is able to do in, for and through us, especially when He gives us the assignment and the tools to search out the land He has placed for us to inhabit. And if the enemy may loom large in our eyes, we can trust that the Lord will never leave nor forsake us. He wants us to be of a good courage and be not afraid or dismayed; for He promises to be with us wherever we go (Joshua 1:9) and will fight the battle on our behalf (Deuteronomy 20:1 and 2 Chronicles 20:15-17). If our walk is upright before God and our desires align with His will, we are sure to have the blessing and guidance of His mighty hand.

We do not know of what lies ahead, but we can be sure that our wise Father God knows and is in full control of what will or will not happen. He has all the bases covered. While we may plan, it is He who will guide our steps and the outcome. Let us not cower to fear, intimidation and uncertainty. We can choose to be a small and insignificant grasshopper and ignore God's promises of great things or we can confidently thrive on his greatness and glory as the fuel that makes us His giants who are ready for the tasks. What would it be?

". . . I come to thee in the name of the Lord of hosts ... The battle is the Lord's (1 Samuel 17:45, 47).

Be Blessed Today in the confidence of who you are in Christ

*I*N TIMES LIKE THESE

The ebb and flow of life's journey can take us to heights and depths of peace, pain, joy, grief. There is a Word for all seasons and for all times – a Word that will not be lost when all else can. A Word fitly spoken in times like these.
Listen! My Beloved.

TODAY

". . . Today if ye will hear His voice, harden not your hearts" (Hebrews 4:7)

Today is the day that God has given us. We have heard that we should live today as the given day for tomorrow is not promised. Scripture teaches that we are not to worry about tomorrow before taking care of today (Matthew 6:34). However, many do live for today with all its extremes and persuasions as though they were indeed no tomorrow.

The word 'Today' as God uses in His holy Scriptures to mean this day, can be viewed as an opportunity or another chance to make the best use of His teaching and of our spiritual journey, to draw close to Him and to cry out for His mercy. Today is a coveted moment in time given to us by God to move from the realm of darkness into His Spirit and light and to understand His perfect will. God was concerned by the rebellion of those who seemed to have a knowledge of Him and yet were so far removed from His truth that He proclaimed them to be of an evil heart and of unbelief in departing from Him and following their own way (Hebrew 3:12). He found it necessary to remind those of us of this day that Today is the day He has given us to hear His voice and we are not to harden our hearts (Psalm 95:7, 8). Today is the day that He has given for us to rejoice and be glad (Psalm 118:24) and to receive our daily bread (Matthew 6:11). Today is the day we work the works of Christ for the night cometh when no man can work (John 9:4).

What we do Today will dictate where we spend tomorrow, in peril or in glorious eternity with Christ. We are cautioned not to pass the time idly but investing in our eternity – soberly, prayerfully, meditating on God's Word and in fellowship with Him, with lives that reflect that we are under the mantle of God's saving grace. Ephesians 5:16 says we are to be redeeming the time because the days are evil.

God's emphasis on Today is His way of extending His mercy to those who will hear His voice, repent and turn from their sin and enter into His rest (Hebrews 3:11). Today is equated with **NOW** and signifies a sense of urgency. Jesus gave immediate eternal promise to the thief on the cross by proclaiming to him that "Today thou shalt be with me in paradise" (Luke 23:43). And God tells us that "Now is the accepted time, now is the day of salvation" (2 Corinthians 6:2), and if we seek Him we shall find Him, if we search for Him with all of our heart (Jeremiah 29:13). Tomorrow is not promised save for Christ's imminent return (if it does not occur today), but Today is given that we be prepared and ready and believing in our hearts all that the Bible has to teach about God, His salvation and eternity. So, **TODAY**, if you will hear His voice, harden not your heart.

"Jesus Christ the same yesterday, and today, and forever" (Hebrews 13:8).

BE BLESSED TODAY

185

*B*ITTER WEEDS

"A merry heart doeth good like a medicine: but a broken spirit drieth the bones" (Proverbs 17:22)

I can't help but recall this song I sang as a child and its message is even fresher and more meaningful to me now than it was then, when it was just a happy melody in a child's ears. "In our dear Lord's garden, planted here below many tiny flowers, in sweet beauty grow. Christ the loving gardener tends each blossom small, loves the little lilies as the cedars tall."[5]

The garden is among the many things that our hearts are likened unto. Yes, the Christian's heart is God's garden and should have room for many blossoming flowers and fruit of the Spirit but not weeds and bush.

So what's growing in our garden? If there are flowers, these are to be watered, cultivated and handled with diligence. But alas, if there are weeds, these must be rooted up and thrown out with great speed. Flowers delight, beautify are fragrant and pleasing and are in the garden as honey for sweetness. Weeds run, grasp, choke, crowd out, interrupt, retard or kill growth and their aroma is pungent. Too often, we are filled with pride and become obsessed with harboring unpleasant experiences, hurt, disappointment, retaliation and unforgiveness.

The long-term result is nothing else but tending a garden overrun with bitter weeds. We can feed these weeds with more resentment, water them with anxiety, and exhibit them with angry, critical and harsh words. The Bible describes this behavior as unprofitable and ascribes it to those who are not righteous or seeking after God and whose mouths are full of cursing and bitterness. (Romans 3:10-14). One's outer garden may appear at times to be well tended, but the inner one of the heart tells a different story and we are advised to guard the heart with all diligence for out of it springs the issues of life (Proverbs 4:23) and this can include the bitter weeds that spring there from.

This is an unfortunate character trait that will raise its ugly head repeatedly and has no place in the Christian's life. The worrisome aspect of this is that it quickly seeps into relationships, erodes the family, pitting one against the other, unsettles the workplace and divides the place of worship as it ferociously takes root and manifests itself in callous behavior, bitter speech, secret ill thoughts and outward displays which are not God-glorifying. It also leaves or creates a bitter taste in the mouths of those affected. Bitter weeds will also rob the Christian of the special joy they have in walking with God from a pure heart and a contented spirit and will grieve the Holy Spirit. The wise counsel of God's Word calls us all to "Let all bitterness and wrath and anger and clamor and evil speaking be put away from you, with all malice" (Ephesians 4:31).

We are to "follow peace with all men, and holiness, without which no man shall see the Lord: looking diligently lest any man fail of the grace of God; lest any root of bitterness springing up trouble you, and thereby many be defiled" (Hebrews 12:14, 15).

As we walk with God day by day, may He have the full run of our hearts, may He direct the flowers that bloom there and perish any ill or bitter weed that may be present.

"And the Lord shall deliver me from every evil work, and will preserve me unto His heavenly kingdom: to whom be glory for ever and ever. Amen" (2 Timothy 4:18).

BE BLESSED TODAY AS A SWEET FRAGRANCE OF LOVE AND KINDNESS

GREETINGS AND SALUTATIONS

"Peace be to the brethren, and love with faith, from God the Father and the Lord Jesus Christ. Grace be with all them that love our Lord Jesus Christ in sincerity. Amen" (Ephesians 6:23, 24)

The Apostle Paul under the inspiration of the Holy Spirit, in writing his epistles and letters always greets his readers, the church, the saints and his sons of the common faith with a message of peace, encouragement and comfort in Christ. His profound words compel the recipient and reader to think on Christ as He testifies of the truth and power of Almighty God who bestows His grace, mercy and salvation to His elect and gives them everlasting peace through Jesus Christ. Paul's greetings are not frivolous, idle or perfunctory, but words of depth, love, life and teaching, warmly penned to embrace awaiting hearts which can in turn reach out and embrace God because they feel loved and cared for and are thankful recipients of His grace and peace.

Paul writes to the beloved of God, called to be saints; ". . . Grace to you and peace from God our Father, and the Lord Jesus Christ. First, I thank my God through Jesus Christ for you . . ." (Romans 1:7, 8). He offers grace and peace from God our Father, and the Lord Jesus Christ, that in every thing we are enriched by Him (God), in all utterance, and in all knowledge (1 Corinthians 1:3-5). With that desire, he also sends his own love and the love of Christ Jesus and the communion of the Holy Ghost to be with our spirits (2 Corinthians 13:14 and Galatians 6:18).

He salutes those who are born again as new creations in Christ and as many as walk according to this rule, peace be on them, and mercy (Galatians 6:16). He cares that their spiritual growth and walk in the Lord would be strengthened and reminds them to be kindly affectioned one to another with brotherly love (Romans 12:10); to be followers of Christ and to walk in love (Ephesians 5:1, 2) and to fulfill the ministry which they have received in the Lord (Colossians 4:17).

In his salutations Paul exhorts all the saints in Christ to stand fast, and hold the traditions which they have been taught, whether by word, or by epistle. He offers reassurance through our Lord Jesus Christ, and God, even our Father, which hath loved us, and hath given us everlasting consolation and good hope through grace. He prays that God would comfort our hearts, and strengthen us in every good word and work (2 Thessalonians 2:16, 17), and that through the comfort of the God of all comfort who comforts us in all our tribulation, that we may be able to comfort them which are in any trouble, by the comfort wherewith we ourselves are comforted of God (2 Corinthians 1:2-4). There is no mistaking that Paul knew God as the source of all wellbeing and desires that we all know and experience that same ease.

Paul's greetings align with God's will. He knows that all he asks and prays for comes from God and so he blesses God and Father of our Lord Jesus Christ who hath blessed us with all spiritual blessings in heavenly places in Christ. (Ephesians 1:3).

He prays for the true believers that the very God of peace sanctify us wholly and our spirit and soul and body to be preserved blameless unto the coming of our Lord Jesus Christ (1 Thessalonians 5:23), and that God would count us worthy of this calling, and fulfill all the good pleasure of His goodness, and the work of faith with power. That the name of the Lord Jesus Christ be glorified in us, and we in Him, according to the grace of our God and the Lord Jesus Christ (2 Thessalonians 1:11, 12).

His prayer and desire is for us to be filled with the knowledge of God's will in wisdom and spiritual understanding and that we might walk worthy of the Lord unto all pleasing, being fruitful in every good work, and increasing in the knowledge of God; and to be strengthened with all might, according to God's glorious power, unto all patience and longsuffering with joyfulness (Colossians 1:9-11). Paul never failed to acknowledge that God's abundant grace was bestowed upon him and he desired the same for others. He thanked God always in every prayer and upon every remembrance of his brethren, making his requests with joy (Philippians 1:3, 4).

As we receive Paul's sincere greetings, salutations and blessings, we should in turn be ready to greet each other with a holy kiss and offer similar words of sincerity, filled with hope, love and instruction to those who are weak, troubled, despairing, perplexed, challenged, forsaken and feeling unloved and faithless in this present age. And even those who are walking in faith; thanking God for them always in our prayer and making supplications with joy on their behalf and we are to do this on every remembrance of them.

Dear friends, I greet you with love and Jesus joy. He is the Alpha and Omega and the greatest joy of our souls and as you honor Him as Lord of all and soon returning King of glory, may He dwell in your hearts by faith; that you being rooted and grounded in love, may be able to comprehend with all saints what is the breadth, and length, and depth, and height; and to know the love of Christ, which passeth knowledge, that ye might be filled with all the fullness of God (Ephesians 3:17-19).

"Now the Lord of peace Himself give you peace always by all means. The Lord be with you all. The grace of the Lord Jesus Christ be with you all. Amen" (2 Thessalonians. 3:16, 18).

BE BLESSED TODAY. GREET ONE ANOTHER IN CHRISTIAN LOVE

Salt and Light

**"Ye are the salt of the earth . . . Ye are the light of the
world . . ." (Matthew 5:13, 14)**

Salt and light are two necessary ingredients in our
lives and it is somewhat difficult to imagine food without salt
and living conditions without light, although some who are
health conscious have salt-free diets and some places have no,
or limited electricity and hence no light.

In Matthew 5: verses 13 and 14, Jesus is speaking to
His disciples and also to true believers everywhere. He gives
us an acknowledgment and an instruction when He says "Ye
are the salt of the earth. Ye are the light of the world." And
when He compares us to salt, He is saying that we have the
responsibility to fulfill His great commission to "go and teach
all nations" (Matthew 28:19). As salt of the earth, the believer
is bearing Christ's character and teaching others about Him
through His Word and by their example. We know that salt
preserves and adds taste and the believer being likened to salt
is called to safeguard and defend the Word of God by their
witness and not dilute or compromise it to accommodate less
faithful doctrines. "For if the salt has lost its savor, wherewith
shall it be salted? It is thenceforth good for nothing but to be
cast out . . ." (Matthew 5:13). In other words Jesus is saying
that if our witness and teaching is not one that upholds the full
counsel of His Word and truthfully declares what the Bible

says and spiritually edifies others, it is therefore useless and fit for nothing.

If we have lost the knowledge of God along the way and haphazardly profess our Christianity and preach anything less than the Gospel, then we are not good for the kingdom of God. As salt of the earth, we are to be preserving Christ's kingdom and the integrity of His Word on this side of heaven until such time as we get there. We are not to be abrasive in our witness, but forthright in speaking of God's judgment on sin and His salvation to those who believe in Him. We are to encourage others to "Taste and see that the Lord is good . . ." (Psalm 34:8), not just as a provider of material goods but as the source of all spiritual blessings through the riches of Christ Jesus. And we have the wherewithal to do so. We have God's Word, His promises, His faith and we are sustained by His grace and the Holy Spirit. As the light of the world, we are emulating Jesus, the great light, who said, ". . . I am the light of the world" (John 9:5); "I am come a light into the world, that whosoever believeth on me should not abide in darkness" (John 12:46).

Jesus is encouraging us as children of His light (Ephesians 5:8) to walk in the light and shine in all the dark places around us and lead others to Him. As He dispels darkness, He is empowering His own to do the same in their daily examples. It is impossible to be a true light and hide it. It is hard to be a Christian and no one notices. We have a grand Gospel story to tell, we have an urgent witness to bear. It must be done in submission to the Christ about whom we are declaring and we are admonished to "let our speech be alway with grace, seasoned with salt, that ye may know how ye ought to answer every man" (Colossians 4:6).

Remarkably, in His discourse, Jesus did not separate the two ingredients salt and light but called our attention to both. He intended that we reflect them both as they truly represent His wonderful personality. As we demonstrate the salt and light of our witness we are not seeking to spread a popular message, but the true and faithful Gospel which shows the great love of God for mankind, that He had to send Jesus to the cross to atone for our sin. May we not lose the superb value and flavor of these two ingredients as we witness for Christ in spirit and in truth.

"Let your light so shine before men, that they may see your good works, and glorify your Father which is in heaven" (Matthew 5:16).

BE BLESSED TODAY WITH THE ZEST AND FLAVOR OF THE GOSPEL OF CHRIST

$\mathcal{T}$HE BIG BAIL OUT

"Herein is love, not that we loved God, but that He loved us, and sent His Son to be the propitiation for our sins" (1 John 4:10)

The talk on the street is all about home foreclosures and bailing out big business that are in trouble and crumbling under enormous bad debt. People are desperately seeking help and have turned their attention to reserves in the hope of being bailed out corporately and individually from these failures, largely due to bad planning, greed and mismanagement. This is the dilemma that presently exists nationally and globally.

We do not have to look too far back in time. History is not that misplaced and Scripture ought not to be forgotten. For one day, not too long ago, mankind was in the predicament of sin and on the brink of doom. At Calvary, the Savior of the world, the Son of God and son of man and our Chief Executive Officer came to the rescue of a dying lot. Weighed down with grief and shame, bearing the burden of, and taking over our sin debts, He performed the most honorable and priceless act of salvation for many dishonorable and unworthy citizens of humanity, you and me.

The big bail out happened at the cross, fulfilling the desires and purpose of a loving Almighty God, who from before the foundation of the world had made this possible (Ephesians 1:4; 2 Thessalonians 2:13), and who commended His love to us, in that, while we were yet sinners, Christ died for us (Romans 5:8). "He was wounded for our transgressions, He was bruised for our iniquities: the chastisement of our peace was upon Him; and with His stripes we are healed" (Isaiah 53:5). He paid our debt and bailed us out with His body and His blood, redeeming us from the clutches of sin and eternal damnation, so that we could be a new and saved creation in Him, called, justified, sanctified and glorified to live unto righteousness in the newness of spirit that He alone provided.

This bail out has no conditions, no clauses, no hidden print of revocation, because we can do nothing to assist or guarantee it. It is perfected in God's love that sought us, His grace that lifted us, His mercy that rescued us and His infinite power and Holy Spirit indwelling that keeps and sustains us.

Why then do we seek to build again the things which Christ destroyed? How then do we turn again to the weak and beggarly elements of sin and greed and desire to be in bondage to such? Have we forgotten the commandment so seek God first and His righteousness and all these things (which He knows we should have and are sufficient for us) will be added to our lives according to His riches in glory by Christ Jesus? (Matthew 6:33; Philippians 4:19). And what about being content with such things as we have? For He promised that He would never leave us nor forsake us (Hebrews 13:5).

For those who would have eyes to see and ears to hear and minds to remember are to take heed of these infallible Words of Scripture which stipulate that "heaven and earth (and the things of the world) shall all pass away but God's Word shall not pass away" (Matthew 24:35). "But godliness with contentment is great gain, for we brought nothing into this world, and it is certain we can carry nothing out" (1 Timothy 6:6, 7). "For the love of money is the root of all evil: which while some coveted after, they have erred from the faith, and pierced themselves through with many sorrows" (1Timothy 6:10). "Man doth not live by bread alone, but by every word that proceedeth out of the mouth of the Lord doth man live" (Deuteronomy 8:3).

Scripture also teaches us that the riches of this world are corrupted (James 5:2), they certainly make wings and fly away (Proverbs 23:5), and "denying ungodliness and worldly lusts, we should live soberly, righteously, and godly, in this present world; looking for that blessed hope, and the glorious appearing of the great God and our Savior, Jesus Christ who gave Himself for us, that He might redeem us from all iniquity, and purify unto himself a peculiar (as His own) people, zealous of good works" (Titus 2:12-14). This same Jesus will once again and very soon bail His chosen ones, out of this wretched world when He returns to rapture those who have been sealed in His grace with the Holy Spirit of promise unto the day of redemption and are living obediently and contented in His provision (Ephesians 1:13).

Meanwhile, we are admonished to "charge them that are rich in this world, that they be not high-minded, nor trust in uncertain riches, but in the living God, who giveth us richly all things to enjoy. That they do good, that they be rich in good works, ready to distribute, willing to share; laying up in store for themselves a good (spiritual) foundation against the time to come, that they may lay hold on eternal life" (1 Timothy 6:17-19).

Let us then be steadfast and faithful stewards, continuing in sound biblical doctrine and pressing toward the mark for the prize of the high calling of God in Christ Jesus (Philippians 3:14), and most definitely consider our ways (Haggai 1:5).

"For what shall it profit a man if he gains the whole world and lose his own soul" (Mark 8:36).

BE BLESSED TODAY AS YOU SEEK NOT YOUR OWN THINGS, BUT THOSE OF CHRIST

GOD'S MOTHERS

**"But when the fullness of time was come, God sent forth
His Son made of a woman . . ." (Galatians 4:4)**

In celebration of mothers, let us thank God for our
own dear mothers and what they mean to us. Let us also thank
him for the biblical mothers Eve, Naomi, Ruth, Hannah,
Sarah, Hagar, Mary, Elizabeth, Eunice, Lois and King
Lemuel's mother of Proverbs 31. They were mothers with
challenges, dreams, desires, fears, anxieties and flaws, but
women who were used by God in a remarkable way to shape
the lives of their children and the course of biblical history.

A mother's job is never done and we are guided to
"train up a child in the way he should go and when he is old he
would not depart from it" (Proverbs 22:6). "The older women
are to be in behavior that becomes holiness, not false accusers,
not given to much wine, teachers of good things and are to
teach the young women to be sober, to love their husbands, to
love their children, to be discreet, chaste, keepers at home,
good, obedient to their own husbands, that the Word of God
be not blasphemed" (Titus 2:3-5).

The Apostle Paul under the inspiration of the Holy
Spirit wrote to Timothy commending his Christian walk "And
that from a child thou hast known the Holy Scriptures, which
are able to make thee wise unto salvation through faith which
is in Jesus Christ" (2 Timothy 3:15). He credited this

upbringing to Timothy's mother, Eunice and grand mother, Lois (2 Timothy 1:5).

God has given mothers an extraordinary role and responsibility of love, caring, nurturing and having a Christian walk and example by which their children can be drawn into the family of the redeemed. A mother cannot give her children salvation, but she is to train and nourish them in the Lord. Her Godly walk can influence and guide her home and the tender hearts therein as she is clothed in strength and honor, wisdom and kindness and looks well to the ways of her household (Proverbs 31:25-27).

No wonder the virtuous woman's children arose up and called her blessed, and not only them but her husband praised her as well (Proverbs 31:28). And so does God.

"Favor is deceitful and beauty is vain, but a woman that fears the Lord, she shall be praised" (Proverbs 31:30).

BE BLESSED TODAY. A GODLY MOTHER IS GOD'S GIFT TO A CHILD

GROWING IN GRACE

Grow

Richly

As

Christ

Exemplifies

And soar to a radiant and fulfilling encounter with the God of Grace.

$\mathcal{A}$ GREAT LESSON

"Teach me O Lord the Way of Thy Statutes . . ." (Psalm 119:33)

We are overtaken today with an abundance of knowledge and information in technology, science and much more. However, there is the lesson of life which God gives us freely and which we are to seek after for deeper knowledge and understanding of His ways. Can we add to our learning a lesson for life that would keep us girded in truth and knowledge for the living of these days in a way that is most pleasing to God?

Therefore, let us like the Psalmist in Psalm 119:33 - 40, ask to be taught the lessons of life and led in the way of truth.

"Teach me, O Lord, the way of Thy Statutes; and I shall keep it unto the end.

Give me understanding, and I shall keep Thy law; yea, I shall observe it with my whole heart.

Make me to go in the path of Thy commandments; for therein do I delight.

Incline my heart unto Thy testimonies, and not to covetousness.

Turn away mine eyes from beholding vanity; and quicken Thou me in Thy way.

Stablish Thy Word unto Thy servant, who is devoted to Thy fear.

203

Turn away my reproach which I fear: for Thy judgments are good.

Behold, I have longed after Thy precepts: Quicken me in Thy righteousness."

When we take hold of such teaching, we will have great experience in wisdom and knowledge that comes forth from the Word of God - our footsteps will not slip, our minds will be renewed, we will not enter into the path of the wicked, nor go in the way of evil men, but walk in everlasting truth.

Get wisdom, get understanding: forget it not, neither decline from the words of My mouth" (Proverbs 4:5).

BE BLESSED TODAY AS YOU SIT AT THE MASTER'S FEET

GIFTS, GIFTS AND MORE GIFTS

"Every good gift and every perfect gift is from above, and cometh down from the Father of lights with whom there is no variableness neither shadow of turning" (James 1:17)

We all like to receive gifts and usually hurry to unwrap them with great excitement and in anticipation of something we would like.

God has given us many wonderful and spiritually satisfying gifts, a fulfillment of His commitment to His elect and these are explained throughout the Scriptures. Let us joyfully unwrap and examine some of them:

The Gift of Grace – God has given us the most wonderful gift of grace and salvation through His son Jesus Christ. "For by grace are ye saved through faith; and that not of yourselves; it is the gift of God" (Ephesians 2:8), and is by one man Jesus Christ (Romans 5:15), and this gift of God is eternal life (Romans 6:23). This gift as all others is free and cannot be worked for, or purchased (Acts 8:20).

The Gift of the Holy Spirit – The believers are baptized of the Holy Spirit who indwells and sustains them during their Christian pilgrimage (Acts 2:38). For as many as are led by the Spirit of God, they are the sons of God. The Spirit beareth witness with our spirit that we are the children of God (Romans 8:14, 16), and will search the deep things of God (1 Corinthians 2:10), and shall teach us all things and bring them to our remembrance (John 14:26). This same Holy

Spirit imparts abundant diverse spiritual gifts to the true believers and these are to be used not for self profit or acclaim, but all to the highest glory of God (1 Corinthians 10:31).

The Gifts of power, love and of a sound mind are an integral part of the true believer's character. They are equipped to think, understand and operate as God wills and demonstrate a life that is grounded in His peace without fear of external forces. "For God hath not given us the spirit of fear; but of power, and of love, and of a sound mind" (2 Timothy 1:7).

The Gifts of prophesy and ministry are given according to the grace that is given to each believer. As we receive these gifts we are to freely administer them in return to the edification and exhortation of the recipients (Romans 12:6-8), speaking in spirit and truth the full counsel of the Word of God.

The Gift of hospitality – As believers we are equipped to share God's Word with others, desiring God's best for them as we do for ourselves. We are called to love our neighbor as we love ourselves and comfort them which are in any trouble, by the comfort wherewith we ourselves are comforted of God (2 Corinthians 1:6). "As every man hath received the gift (of hospitality), even so minister the same one to another, as good stewards of the manifold grace of God" (1 Peter 4:9). Added to this, every man should eat and drink and enjoy the good of all his labor, it is the gift of God (Ecclesiastes 3:13).

The Gift of prayer is given to all believers. Jesus taught his disciples and us to pray, that means talking to God. So we are to pray for ourselves and one for another. "Is any among you afflicted? Let him pray . . ." (James 5:13). ". . . The effectual fervent prayer of a righteous man availeth much" (James 5:16). We are to pray without ceasing (1 Thessalonians 5:17). Men are to pray everywhere (1 Timothy 2:8), and do so not with feigned lips (Psalm 17:1) but from the heart in all sincerity. For if we regard iniquity in our heart the Lord will not hear our prayer (Psalm 66:18).

The Gift of peace – This is a wonderful gift of ease and contentment in God's provision and care given to believers who know and confess the beauty of God's peace which surpasses all understanding and keeps their hearts and minds (in all situations) through Christ Jesus who said "Peace I leave you, My peace I give unto you" (Philippians 4:7 and John 14:27). By virtue of this precious gift, believers are able to follow after the things which make for peace, and things wherewith one may edify another (Romans 14:19).

Do we recognize the gifts of God, and how are we using them? Proverbs 17:8 tell us that a gift is a precious stone in the eyes of him that have it: wherever it turns, it prospers. Are we using these precious stones to their full potential? Are we blessing and edifying others and serving God's kingdom well? Are we bringing our gifts, the best fruit of our lives to God's altar? We are to be careful not to neglect the gifts that are within us, but stir up the gift of God which is in us to prosper in the way God desires and most of all we are to covet earnestly the best gifts, as God shows us the more excellent way which is in Christ Jesus (1 Corinthians 12:31).

**"Thanks be unto God for His unspeakable Gift"
(2 Corinthians 9:15).**

BE BLESSED TODAY AND USE YOUR GIFTS WELL

$\mathcal{T}$HE POOR IN SPIRIT

"Blessed are the poor in spirit for theirs is the kingdom of heaven" (Matthew 5:3)

Jesus used every opportunity to teach people including His disciples and to impart His Words of truth and encouragement. On one such occasion as he gave His sermon on the mount also known as the Beatitudes, Jesus spoke with great compassion on the state of the poor. Among the many who sought him out were the poor. They followed him at great length to get a glimpse of Him, hear Him speak and witness His great miracles. "The blind received their sight and the lame walk, the lepers are cleansed and the deaf hear, the dead are raised up and the poor have the Gospel preached to them" (Matthew 11:5).

Once while Jesus was in the temple, He looked up and saw the rich men casting their gifts into the treasury and He also saw a certain poor widow casting in her two mites (Luke 21:1, 2). He was particularly moved to single out this poor woman because in comparison to those who gave of their abundance, she gave out of the poverty of her purse and the generosity of her spirit, all that she possessed. Similarly, the lad with the two loaves and five fish willingly gave all that he had to feed the hungry and Jesus blessed and multiplied this paltry meal to feed and satisfy thousands (see Luke Chapter 9).

We are not to confuse being poor materially with being poor in spirit. The former speaks to a lack of material means and the latter is the acknowledgment of our spiritual inadequacy, our being broken, contrite and open for God's filling. It is seen in our total reliance on God's grace and our need of Him in all aspects of our lives, particularly in the receiving of His Word with faith and obedience. God declares ". . . To this man will I look, even to him that is poor and of a contrite spirit, and trembleth at My Word" (Isaiah 66:2). And Jesus uses the examples above to illustrate this teaching. The Apostle Paul knew something about being poor in spirit. He acknowledged that he knew how to be abased and to abound, he was instructed both to be full and to be hungry, to abound and to suffer need (Philippians 4:12). He also knew that God's grace was totally sufficient for him (2 Corinthians 12:9). He was not referring to material possessions or edible food but the meat of the Word in that the more he received it, the more he wanted it.

Scripture carefully points out that a man's life consists not of the abundance of what he has (Luke 12:15), because he can have much and yet be poor spiritually and he can have little and be spiritually rich. Lazarus, a certain beggar had nothing in life but sores and the desire to be fed with the crumbs from the rich man's table, but in death found himself eternally rich, being escorted by the angels into Abraham's bosom (Luke 16:19-31). God surely was his helper and his salvation. "Better is the poor that walks in his uprightness than the perverse though he be rich" (Proverbs 28:6).

Being poor in spirit is nothing to be ashamed of, it is to be an endearing quality of the Christian. We can never know enough of God that we cannot learn more from His Word. We can never be so impatient with and judgmental of other's failings without acknowledging that "by the grace of God, there go I." We cannot be so self-serving that we fail to serve others, taking Jesus' example and Words to heart, "the Son of man came not to be ministered unto, but to minister, and to give his life a ransom for many" (Matthew 20:28). "For ye know the grace of our Lord Jesus Christ, that, though He was rich, yet for our sakes He became poor, that ye through His poverty might be rich" (2 Corinthians 8:9).

For God raises up the poor out of the dust (1 Samuel 2:8). He saves them from the sword and the hand of the mighty (Job 5:15). He delivers them from their affliction (Job 36:15). He hears their cries and saves them out of all their troubles (Psalm 34:6), and in all these dispositions we can agree that they that are well have no need of a physician and our expectation is of God (Psalm 62:5).

God requires us to have a certain personality or character that is broken before Him and open for His blessings. The poor in spirit is such a one and to these He ascribes "Blessed". In other words they are saved, well off, fortunate and highly favored. And to the poor in spirit is promised the kingdom of heaven. What a treasure! We are,

211

therefore, to take the Words of Scripture seriously and "seek first the kingdom of God and His righteousness" and trust Him for the blessing that He promises (Matthew 6:33).

"Hearken my beloved brethren, hath not God chosen the poor of this world, rich in faith, and heirs of the kingdom which He hath promised to them that love Him?"
(James 2:5).

BE BLESSED TODAY AND LET THE POOR SAY I AM RICH

Grow as you go

"And these are they which are sown on good ground; such as hear the Word, and receive it, and bring forth fruit, some thirty fold, some sixty and some an hundred" (Mark 4:20)

"Then he that had received the five talents went and traded with the same, and made them other five talents" (Matthew 25:16)

There are many significant lessons that we can glean from these two parables - the sower and the seed and the talents. In these earthly stories with heavenly meanings, the recipients of God's Word which is portrayed by the seed which the sower sows and the talent which the traveler gives to his servants, are all given the opportunity to mature and grow in the Lord and not be useless or stagnated by fear, habits or self-will. Some used it well, others did not.

Sometimes in our own walk and witness, there can be some uncertainty or hesitancy to fully submerging ourselves in God's Word, putting it to work effectively in our lives and witnessing to others. We can feel inadequate with words, talent or offerings; we may misunderstand the purpose of God's plan for our lives, or be unsure of our own spiritual direction and maturity in the Word and conclude that who we are or what we do is not perfect enough to count for Christ. Let us not stumble, falter, be timid or misguided by our own accounts but accept the wonderful opportunity that Christ has given us to spread His Word, minister in His name and study

213

to show ourselves approved unto Him rightly dividing the Word of truth (2 Timothy 2:15), and to grow in His grace. We are commissioned to go and teach all nations and to grow as we go with Christ's blessed promise to be with us alway, even unto the end of the world (Matthew 28:19, 20). We have a wonderful, caring, forgiving and exemplary Savior who is with us every step of the way.

God used many souls from humble and sometimes tainted and flawed beginnings, showing them as He does us, the more excellent way to faithfulness, commitment, knowing, going and growing. Take for example, Moses who was slow in speech and greatly intimidated by his assignment to represent God before the Pharaoh and lead the Israelites out of Egypt. God used him mightily with the help of his brother Aaron to fulfill this task and train them in the ways of the Lord as they sojourned 40 years in the wilderness. Moses used the Word of God (the Ten Commandments) and the presence of God to grow on the job. He equipped Joshua to walk in his footsteps and he was not at all hesitant to carry the mantle – he grew along the journey.

The disciples were a spiritually inexperienced crew from diverse backgrounds, but as they walked with Jesus, watched him keenly and listened to His teachings, they grew from strength to strength as they followed him. They moved from doubt, power struggles and insecurity to being sent out two by two. Peter emerged from catching fish and grew through many hard lessons of impetuousness and rugged pride to catching men for Christ. Saul, the persecutor of the Christian church, turned Paul the Apostle by God's touch, was transformed from a scholarly nuisance to a spiritual giant and missionary and was used tremendously by God to eloquently script His Word. John Mark in the beginnings of his missionary journey with Paul and Barnabas was unreliable and inexperienced and was dropped from the team but Paul later found him to be profitable and of great use for the ministry (2 Timothy 4:11). And Scripture tells us that Jesus, as a lad, increased in wisdom and stature and in favor with God and man. His own earthly parents were amazed at His delivery in the temple (Luke 2:46-52).

Can we, like Mary (Martha & Lazarus' sister) recognize that which is needful and sit at the Master's feet and hear His Word and choose that good part which shall not be taken away? How can we grow, if we do not know? How can we know if we do not feed on God's Word, precept upon precept, line upon line, here a little, and there a little (Isaiah 28:10), and be committed to learning its truth and diligently obeying same as the litmus of our testimony. Then being confident of this very thing that He (God) which began a good work in us will perform it until the day of Jesus Christ (Philippians 1:6).

"Moreover it is required in stewards that a man be found faithful" (1 Corinthians 4:2).

"For everyone that useth milk is unskillful in the Word of righteousness: for he is a babe. But strong meat belongeth to them that are of full age . . ." (Hebrews 5:13, 14).

BE BLESSED TODAY AND BE SURE TO GROW AS YOU GO

MOVING FROM MILK TO MEAT

"When I was a child, I spake as a child, I understood as a child, I thought as a child: but when I became a man, I put away childish things" (1 Corinthians 13:11)

These thoughts are a continuation of the previous study entitled "Grow as you Go" and are extended to include the ingredients of milk and meat as biblically portrayed to mean the weaning and growing stages of our spiritual lives, the difference between an immature step and a seasoned Christian walk, and from which the title of this publication is inspired. We all know that we feed infants milk for a period of time before we wean them off to solid foods. As they grow and are ready for this transition, if we were to continue feeding them with milk, their physical growth will be severely impeded. Similarly, as Christians our spiritual growth must be fully nurtured, encouraged and strengthened through all stages with the appropriate spiritual food, if not we will be stagnated, barren and unfruitful.

Scripture teaches that newborn babes, (i.e. new Christians) desire the sincere milk of the Word, that ye may grow thereby (1 Peter 2:2) as the first stage to learning about God. We begin by walking through His Word, desiring to know its truths and we put those truths to work in our lives. However, God expects more from us than being baby Christians. As we study His Word and it becomes rooted in us, we are to have a reaction to it and the Holy Spirit indwelling us which shows that we understand doctrine. "Whom shall he teach knowledge? And whom shall he make to understand doctrine? them that are weaned from the milk, and drawn from the breasts" (Isaiah 28:9).

It is essential that we hold fast to sound doctrine and not stagger at its truth or faint in our walk or wander for lack of meat. It is God's desire that we be strengthened with all teaching and enriched by His grace, although sometimes we can fall short or take a longer time to transition from milk to the sincere meat of the Word. For when for the time ye ought to be teachers, ye have need that one teach you again which be the first principles of the oracles of God; and are become such as need of milk, and not of strong meat. Let us not park at the milk can for longer than is needed. "For everyone that useth milk is unskillful in the Word of righteousness: for he is a babe" (Hebrews 5:13).

Jesus is teaching us that we are not to linger too long on our childish faith but move to the full age of learning of, and living for Him and adding to our faith virtue; and to virtue knowledge (2 Peter 1:5), and that we might be filled with the knowledge of His will in all wisdom and spiritual understanding (Colossians 1:9). Strong meat belongs to them that are of full age, even those who by reason of use have their senses exercised to discern both good and evil (Hebrews 5:14).

He reminds those who are lingering behind that He has meat to eat that they know not of (John 4:32), and cautions us all to be careful in our quest for knowledge of Him, not to labor for the meat that perishes (John 6:27). This means we are not to follow after strange doctrines or embrace unholy life styles, rather we are to be workmen worthy of our meat (Matthew 10:10) having the understanding, knowledge and depth of God's Word that will be seen in our effectual testimony of faith, our witness to others and bringing forth fruit unto God. In other words, God wants His family of elect to be rooted and grounded in Him, His Word and established in His faith, and to be a peculiar (His own design) people, zealous of good works, having been filled to all overflowing and walking in all newness of life.

"The eyes of all wait upon Thee (God) and Thou givest them their meat in due season" (Psalm 145:15).

BE BLESSED TODAY, NURTURED AND FILLED WITH THE MEAT OF THE GOSPEL

ROOTED AND GROUNDED IN LOVE

"That Christ may dwell in your hearts by faith; that ye, being rooted and grounded in love, may be able to comprehend with all saints what is the breadth, and length, and depth, and height; and to know the love of Christ which passeth knowledge, that ye might be filled with all the fullness of God" (Ephesians 3:17-19)

The words rooted and grounded convey the idea of stability, fortitude, strength, permanency, confidence. In Ephesians Chapter 3 the Apostle Paul under the inspiration of the Holy Spirit, writes to the church at Ephesus about God's purpose for their salvation and the love of Christ toward the Gentiles, which are framed in longevity, permanency, faithfulness, truth, eternity and without end.

Paul himself was rooted and grounded in the full knowledge and grace of God with the assurance that he was saved and called to preach among the Gentiles the unsearchable riches of Christ. He considered himself less than the least of all saints who benefitted greatly from God's manifold grace (Ephesians 3:8). He did not hesitate to tell others of his great love for Christ, his commitment to bring the Gospel to the unsaved and of his desire that the whole family of God would know of, and understand the love of Christ, and be granted inner strength to live purposely for God, having been saved by grace through faith and raised up to sit together in heavenly places in Christ Jesus (Ephesians 2:6, 8).

Those of us, who have received Christ, should like Paul, bow our knees unto the Father of our Lord Jesus Christ, and eagerly receive His Word as true and faithful and thank Him for his transforming power which is able to bring us into the unity of the faith and of the knowledge of the Son of God. It is good wisdom that we continue in the faith, grounded and settled, and be not moved away from the hope of the Gospel of Christ. We are reminded that in all these things we are more than conquerors through Christ that loved us. Being fully persuaded that nothing can separate us from His love, not even height or depth - the immeasurable dimensions of our relationship with Christ and His with us. In Christ's love, we are no longer aliens, strangers and foreigners, but fellow-citizens with the saints and of the household of God, heirs of God and joint heirs with Christ (Ephesians 2:19; Romans 8:17).

There is no time like now to renew our determination to search and know the holy Scriptures which testify of Christ (John 5:39), to be nourished by its Words which are able to make us wise unto salvation, through faith which is in Christ Jesus, and to remain rooted and grounded and built up in God and established in the faith, as we have been taught, abounding therein with thanksgiving. With such a resolve and purpose, no man can spoil us through philosophy and vain deceit. We are complete in God, which is the head of all principality and power (Colossians 2: 7-10).

"As ye have therefore received Christ Jesus the Lord, so walk ye in Him" (Colossians 2:6).

BE BLESSED TODAY FIRMLY ANCHORED IN CHRIST

*R*EADY, WILLING AND ABLE

"Have not I commanded thee? Be strong and of a good courage; be not afraid, neither be thou dismayed: for the Lord thy God is with thee wherever thou goest"
(Joshua 1:9)

Joshua Chapter 1 introduces the story of a time and place when Joshua was left with a great and awesome responsibility to lead the Israelites into the Promised Land after the death of Moses. It was a daunting task, it was of enormous proportion, but from the inception, God promised Joshua favor. He promised him that He will never leave him nor forsake him. He will equip him for the journey. He will prepare him. He will make him ready, willing and able.

God has that same message for us. We have great desires and ambitions of service, and we want to please God with our walk, and yet, there are times obstacles may hinder our response. In the midst of our daily lives, God is singling each of us out to the awesome task of walking with Him and serving Him. Is it our intent to be ready, willing and able to respond? God has that same message for us that He gave Joshua. If we look at verses 6, 7 and 8 we will find the tools He is providing to make us ready willing and able:

1) Be Strong and of good courage (vs. 6)

2) Be Strong and very courageous (vs. 7)

2) Do not waver or be swayed (vs. 7)

3) Stay in and live the Word (vs. 8)

God instructs Joshua that the book of the law, which is God's Word, shall not depart out of his mouth; but he should meditate on it day and night and follow its instructions. Meditate means to read, study, chew it inside out, ponder it, and then do it. Not only does God speak of these tools, but He gives them to us. He has given us His Word, He has given us courage in Him, as we read in many Psalms where David declares that God indeed is his strength, his courage, his expectation, his high tower, his safety net (see Psalm 18:1, Psalm 27:1, Psalm 62:1-7). The key, therefore, to being ready, willing and able is to stay grounded in God's Word, and be obedient to it and we will find by doing so, we will be spiritually effective and we can safely and confidently affirm:

I am ready because I am walking in the Spirit to overcome the ills of the flesh (John 3:6 and Galatians 5:16).

I am ready because God has prepared me through the cleansing blood of His Son and my Savior, Jesus Christ. (Romans 3:25).

I am willing because I am being led by the Holy Spirit and my will is surrendered to God, therefore, it is not my will, but God's will be done (Luke 11:2).

I am willing not with eye service, as men pleasers; but as the servant of Christ, doing the will of God from the heart (Ephesians 6:6).

I am able because I can do all things through Christ who gives me strength (Philippians 4:13).

I am able because God is able to keep me from falling (Jude 1:24).

I am able because God is able to do exceeding abundantly above all that I ask or think, according to the power that worketh in me (Ephesians 3:20).

I am able because the Lord God is my strength, and He will make my feet like hinds' feet, and He will make me to walk upon my high places (Habakkuk 3:19).

We can trust God because His Word is reliable, His character is dependable and His power is inexhaustible. He will not fail us, disappoint us, forsake us, ignore us nor forget us. And because He abides in us and we abide in him we can declare victoriously that we are ready, willing and able as He has blessed and strengthened us to be about His business.

And if we feel this is lacking in our lives, it is not too late to pray for it. We can have a little talk with Jesus on this and any other matter that rests on our heart today. We are not to be anxious for anything, but in everything, with prayer and supplication, and with thanksgiving make our requests known to God and the peace of God that passeth all understanding will keep our hearts and minds through Christ Jesus (Philippians 4:6, 7).

"This book of the law shall not depart out of thy mouth;
but thou shall meditate therein day and night, that thou
may observe to do according to all that is written therein:
for then thou shall make thy way prosperous, and then
thou shall have good success" (Joshua 1:8).

BE BLESSED TODAY IN ALL READINESS TO SERVE GOD

References

1)   Hymn "Christ the Lord is Risen Today" by Charles Wesley, 1707-1788.
2)   Hymn "God Will Take Care of You" by Civilla D. Martin and W. Stillman Martin, 1869 – 1948.
3)   Hymn "Loves Divine All Loves Excelling" by Charles Wesley, 1707-1788.
4)   Hymn "Turn Your Eyes Upon Jesus" by Helen H. Lemmel, 1922.
5)   Hymn "In Our Dear Lord's Garden" by E.S. Armitage, 1841-1931.